Habits

How Leaders Shape Stories That Drive Action

(Rewire Your Brain to Build Better Habits and Unlock Your Full Potential)

Priscilla Scherer

Published By **Oliver Leish**

Priscilla Scherer

Habits: How Leaders Shape Stories That Drive Action (Rewire Your Brain to Build Better Habits and Unlock Your Full Potential)

ISBN   978-1-77485-985-8

Legal & Disclaimer

The information contained in this ebook is not designed to replace or take the place of any form of medicine or professional medical advice. The information in this ebook has been provided for educational & entertainment purposes only.

The information contained in this book has been compiled from sources deemed reliable, and it is accurate to the best of the Author's knowledge; however, the Author cannot guarantee its accuracy and validity and cannot be held liable for any errors or omissions. Changes are periodically made to this book. You must consult your doctor or get professional medical advice before using any of the suggested remedies, techniques, or information in this book.

TABLE OF CONTENTS

Chapter 1: Be Clear In Your Thoughts

What is the one thing in your life that makes you have a strong desire to possess? What is the emotion you are certain makes you feel the most content and happy and leave all your rational thinking aside? Perspectives play an important aspect in determining the type of success you want. Since the first day they are able to recall, the majority of people around the world have received directions on how they can do things. This is why it is that people are difficult to figure out what they want in life.

Being able to think clearly is crucial to achieve your goals and aspirations. You can invest time in understanding the things that are most crucial to you succeed in life , if you possess the ability to think clearly. It is essential to have a clear idea of the goals you wish to achieve. The objectives should be clear to ensure there is no any doubt about the best way to accomplish them. Once you've decided to set a goal will you be able to dedicate more effort and time to it. Look at Michael Jordan or Serena Williams both of whom have received numerous awards throughout their careers. One thing they share in the same way is that they were both convinced of their goals in their lives. It was due to their clear idea that they began an intense journey to attain the highest level of excellence. The more precise your vision of what you're looking for and the more straightforward it will be to focus on it with out any distraction.

What is the reason that clarity of thought Relevance?

A clear and precise sense of direction is vital because a confused mind and indecisiveness could cause more worries and problems than they are able to resolve. The process of setting goals isn't as simple as it appears to be. Priorities and perspectives are crucial in determining what is successful. While certain people excel in science, while others are successful in arts however, their definition of success might differ in a radical way.

Transparency of thought is essential to determining what is important and essential to you. For example, Barack Obama achieved one of the top places in the world. In order to make that goal achievable, he had to begin with an objective view. With a clear and concise idea, the determination to it will be steadfast and that is an excellent benefit for success.

A clear and focused mind is vital to live a meaningful and productive life. It is also beneficial to develop the great habit of clearing one's mind of distractions , and to focus on a single goal into practice.

What are some vague goals?

Vague goals are an unfulfilled idea of something that you wish to have. For instance, you could declare that you would like to make lots of money. But, "earning a lot of money" is an undefined goal because it is essential to be able to determine the exact amount you'd like to earn and at what time. Think about the following scenario It is that you wish to shed weight, but what amount of ounces or pounds? Do you wish to lose weight and achieve your ideal BMI or do you simply want to slim down just a few inches? Another instance is an executive who announces that he will increase his followers on social media across all his accounts. The question remains how many? These types of thoughts are considered to have a vague mental state. If you're not clear on your goals in your life, you'll be unable to accomplish your goals.

One of the best method to stay clear of unclear objectives is to have a solid understanding within the field where you want to excel. If you wish to become an effective scientist, it is essential to decide on the area of science that you would like to be a specialist in. In the end your primary goal is to learn about a specific area, like Chemistry or physics. It is important to be sure of what you're comfortable doing the rest of your time studying. Your dedication and commitment must be constant and never change..

Whatever career path you pick being clear about your decision is the most crucial element in your future success. If you've set out to reach your goals, then you cannot afford to be unsure of the direction you take. You must be certain of what you'd like to achieve in your life, and that belief alone will keep you focused until you reach your goals.

The lack of clarity in your thoughts can affect your goals

Have you ever considered if your notion of success might be somewhat unclear and how it might influence your career opportunities? It is true that everyone is a bit unsure and distracted all the time. Your mind can operate in ways you're incapable of understanding. It is possible to feel self-confident on certain days, and depressed in others. The fundamental concept is that it's your responsibility to improve yourself, and especially your mind by incorporating a few beneficial practices into your routine. It is essential to comprehend the reason why clarity of thinking is essential for the long-term. Also, you can look at the following essential elements to understand the ways that the lack of clarity of thinking can hinder your goals over the long term:

A confused mind could result in a reversal within your thought.

When you're thinking in hazy thoughts You'll be confused that prevents you from making sure you take the right steps.

A lack of clarity hinders you from implementing clear strategies. * You delay more because of confusion.

* You won't be aware of the tasks that will can help you become more successful.

• Developing the behaviors that will help you achieve your goals will be an arduous task.

* And, perhaps most frighteningly is the thought that you should quit because of mental clarity.

In the end as a result, you need to be able to recognize what your true goal is for success. Make sure your mind is clear, to be in a position achieve your goals with determination.

Why is it important to set clear Goals?

Nearly everyone is driven by a sense of success. A lot of people, regardless of their gender, age and age are driven by the idea of having control over their lives. But, not many people are aware that having a rapid mind leads to more anxiety and, in many instances there is a lot of frustration and stress.

If you believe in the possibility that you can achieve what you want the majority of your issues are resolved. Here are a few of the reasons why having clear goals are essential to be successful:

* You'll know exactly what you'd like to achieve in your life when you are in clarity. The way you approach and the steps you take are determined by the plan you have in mind. You'll know the behaviors you'll need to build to accomplish your goals.

* You're more focused and driven.

If you are aware of what you'd like then you'll be able to establish a time frame that you'll be working for your objectives.

Imagine embarking on the space journey and not sure if you want to just circle the orbit , or make it to the moon half way through. Although this scenario might seem, you need to be aware that your vision and focus should be clear and precise. You will only be able to achieve your goals when you are honest and` have clear thinking. Thus, having certain goals will most likely improve your chances of being successful.

How can you incorporate this Habit?

It's as obvious as it could be it is true that one thing is for certain that successful people rise to the top because being able to see rationally and clearly. If you're seeking ways to increase your vision clarity to be successful Here are a few strategies:

The Manifest

Take note of what your top goal is and then plan to get there as soon as you are able. Consider your hopes and dreams Consider whether you'd like to become a well-known novelist, scientist, politician or a baker for example. Consider what you're seeking. A lot of people believe that manifesting is an incredibly powerful force. A method where you want something so strongly that you are focused on getting it. If you follow a certain form that follows the laws that attracts you, it's possible to get the things you've been working to achieve. After you've established what you'd like to achieve for your future, you're able to manifest it in various ways. A constant belief and determination in your abilities to achieve can greatly contribute for your success overall. Only when you think in a clear and focused manner can you succeed. Positive thoughts will help you and you'll be able to bring more positivity to your life.

Motivational Yourself

The importance of determining the goal you want to achieve cannot be overemphasized. If you are aware of the goal you are after and know what you want, you will be able to determine the factors that will keep you focused over time to achieve it. In the cold winter morning simply getting up from your winter blanket and rushing to get the bottle of water sitting on the table may be a challenge and require a lot. Different people have different goals and their motivational styles are different. Decide what is most important to you, and then the several factors that aid you in focusing your efforts.

Take a look at the people you consider to be best in the field, study their methods and discover the path they took to get to where they are now. Consider their role as a source of inspiration. Reread and reflect on their successes every time you fall short and lose the drive to achieve success. Their stories have many stories and lessons you can identify with and, by knowing the way they fought their circumstances, you'll be motivated beyond your imagination. If they're able to do it, why shouldn't you? It is not easy to overlook hard work however, to remain on the same path for a long duration, it takes an enormous amount of motivation. Set your sights on the goal and ensure that it is impossible for distractions to deter you from your steadfast determination. It's your responsibility to find the motivation you need to encourage you to develop healthier habits and grow after you've established a goal for yourself.

Create an Expiration Date

Don't just set your sights; make plans for the time when you'll achieve your goals. The amount of time you allow yourself will determine the intensity of your work toward your target. For instance, you could commit to a whole year to complete a book, however, should you have the opportunity you could complete the same thing within a few months. This is the plan strategy that you must implement in order to reach your long-term goals. Making deadlines and reminders will increase your confidence and serve as a roadmap to follow your plan.

Making deadlines is among the most essential habits you should be able to succeed. Making a list of reminders and trying to finish the task within a certain time frame are two highly efficient abilities that you must work to improve. If you're given deadlines to resolve a problem or tackle a problem that you're working on, you'll be more engaged. You'll be more driven to finish your work on time in the event that you know you have to finish your task within a set time. When you have deadlines in mind, you'll feel pressured to complete your work in a timely manner and the most crucial thing you'll learn is how important it is to manage your time. As you progress, you'll learn to recognize the impact of time on every aspect of your life and be able to make the best utilization of your time because of it. Additionally, you'll be able to realize how having clearly defined goals can help you in many different ways.

If it's shares or stocks the time of every second is important, and the importance of time is paramount in every aspect of our professional as well as in personal lives. Therefore by establishing the habit of setting clear deadlines and goals for yourself, you'll improve as a professional and as an individual. You'll also be able understand how setting clear goals will benefit you in numerous ways.

Relax and relax.

There are times when you set goals for yourself , but fall short of reaching it. The constant competition everyone faces in their careers can cause you to feel vulnerable and anxious sometimes, which can make it difficult to concentrate. If you're overwhelmed by the tasks to handle You'll see how relaxing an environment that is calm can be. Don't dwell on your successes or mistakes in this period. This will result in peace that you can achieve through silence can be a great benefit.

Everyone must recognize that it is important to take a little time to unwind and clear their minds of unneeded thoughts. Yoga and breathing exercises will assist you. Use as many techniques as you want and breath with complete concentration to let your mind go. The holidays and vacations aren't to be ignored and taking time off from work could be a great opportunity to let your thoughts go. Stress from everyday life can create an obstruction in your brain and make your job more challenging. Be aware of the situations in which you begin to realize you're overworked and require to relax. Make sure you take a solitary break and make a promise to yourself that you'll come back more energized than you were the previous. It is beneficial for your overall health and will assist you in working more efficiently and be more productive over the long term. There are a variety of methods one could try to attain an atmosphere of tranquility and peace. Make the most of every opportunity to relax and focus on your ultimate goal.

With the aid by this particular method of clearing your mind of the things you are looking for and why you want it, you'll be able to understand the reasons and how you intend to succeed in your life. To succeed you need to be agile and clear in your thinking. A constant state of mind will not only help you succeed in your profession and will assist you in understanding various concepts with more clarity. If you're feeling down, consider your goals and ways to inspire yourself. Be sure to state clearly that you'll do your best and achieve your goals within a certain timeframe. Make sure that you are driven to reach your goals. Get rid of the agitation from your mind and fill it with rational and positive thoughts.

Chapter 2: Concentration On Growth

We've heard about "focus" from our instructors and coaches, parents, and even our friends since the time we were children. Many of us know what it means to be focused, but few people can stress the importance of it in any level of development either in a professional or personal. If you look at some of the most interview and quote quotes of successful individuals you'll see how much emphasis they place on the word 'focus.'

Apple Inc.'s co-founder Apple Inc., once stated , "People think focus means accepting the thing you have to be focused on. It's not really what it really means. It's about refusing to accept the hundreds of other ideas that are. It is important to choose carefully." This is a simple explanation The focus you set on a particular target is what will determine the outcome of its the success of or its failure. It requires a lot effort to map out your route to reach it. Every effort that you invest in something is never wasted and you either win either way, or in the worst case scenario, you fall short, but the knowledge gained can help you succeed.

A constant focus on your goals will aid you in achieving success. Focus is among the most crucial traits that anyone who is successful anywhere in the world could boast about. The issue is how to remain focus?

This is a pulsing atmosphere brimming with amazing people, opportunities, new ideas, and other fascinating aspects. What can keep you focused and focused on your goal in this kind of circumstance? It's possible to learn plenty by studying the success stories of individuals you've always admired. For instance, Elon Musk, a successful business magnate who owns Tesla and SpaceX is a great growth case. If you study his growth chart, you'll be able to see that he is committed to his goals through any difficulties. He has surpassed all obstacles and set an amazing model for all by being focused and working hard to achieve goals that seem impossible to achieve. He is a pioneer in the realm of revolutionizing transport, both on Earth as well as in space. Everyone knows about his Tesla automobiles and his amazing SpaceX missions.

Elon spent his childhood with his family in South Africa before moving to Canada at the age of 17. As an exchange student, he enrolled at in the University of Pennsylvania. In spite of numerous ups and downs during his time there was one thing that stood out: his ability to keep working towards continuous improvement. It is because of this habit that he's now one of the greatest entrepreneurs. From being a typical student at a transfer school within the United States to now owning an $74 billion company is an experience that will motivate many who get too focused on themselves and believe that they won't ever succeed in any goal. So, be a champion for yourself and concentrate on the work you do to make your dreams come closer to your heart.

Tips to Improve Your Focus

In order to be able to complete your task successfully, you need to be in complete concentration. If you don't pay attention to what you are looking for and focusing on what you want, you won't be able to focus. There will be moments where your attention span is going to decrease. Anyone can concentrate but a strong brain should be developed so that you keep clear of distractions. Because distractions are all in our daily lives! If you are determined to achieve your goals, you must recognize the importance of using different methods to be focused on your goals. Here are a few strategies to instill this wonderful habit of focusing on your growth:

Engage Your Mind

Your attitude is key to helping you become stronger and more focused. What you put into your mind will determine the result. You are positive if you are optimistic and are able to find solutions to issues. Certain people, on the other hand, spot imperfections in the most ideal of situations. They tend to be hard to be around and can spread negativity wherever they travel. It is a negative feeling being around people who have such mindsets. The ability to activate your mind is essential for healthy growth and achievement. The goal you set should be clear and no negative thoughts is allowed to block your way towards success. Positive attitude can make the toughest situations manageable.

The process of learning can be overwhelming and you'll have a lot of assumptions that may or may not be the truth or aren't necessary to grow. Be aware of the aspects you have to alter and what you must improve your skills to stay ahead of the competitors in your field. Be aware of your surroundings and attempt to identify what is your primary goal and the reason you require it to be successful. There are a variety of ways to keeping your mind alert and clear.

Do whatever you can to help keep your mind calm whether that's meditation or taking a relaxing stroll. Create small mental exercises to to recharge your batteries. Your mind and body are always in sync. It is important to take a few minutes to relax whenever you need to get back to health. Music can be a wonderful source of support when you're suffering from an eerie mind. You can listen to music that you likeand then slowly you'll notice that the agitation in your head will wear off very easily. Playing brain games, like is not just a way to prevent you from wasting your time with useless thoughts but also test your mind's capabilities. The goal is to attain the state of mind that is alert and conscious of what you would like to achieve and what you wish to think about, and, most importantly, what you'll need to do to attain the success you've always wanted to achieve.

Beware of What Distracts You

Have you considered finishing the painting or task you set out to complete some time ago however the buzz of social media is making you feel distracted? Distractions can impede our progress or make it difficult to do the things we planned to accomplish. For example, you might have a plan to go to Bali but when you look online for information about different travel packages available, a lot of pop-ups continue to appear as ads that recommend you go towards Thailand instead. This situation presents an issue of which option to select, and can deter you from reaching your original desired destination.

The idea of distraction works well with the concept of marketing. What you find appealing may be the result of a campaign that successfully distracts you. Because of your indecisiveness marketers can benefit from realizing their goals. For instance, you're at a mall and you come across the aisle that contains vegetable oils. When you begin searching through the racks to determine which oil to choose and you are greeted with questions about the store and their service.

Distractions come in many kinds and sizes, it's your responsibility to discover what irritates you most. It's your total control. Imagine a different scenario that you're a huge foodie and are sitting in your study area to work on your class when you smell the aroma of freshly baked cakes nearby. It may seem trivial to some, however your attention is distracted for a while due to your sense of the smell. The result is that you waste the time you could have used to accomplish something that will benefit your overall development instead of searching to find the perfect cake, or contemplating the cake. It is important to realize that distractions can linger in your mind and lead you away from what your real goal might be. Be cautious of what could end up being an unnecessary expense of your time and energy. Be aware and consider your options before you engage in any activity that you are doing, and then ask yourself if the action you take will be worthwhile or not. When you do this you'll be able to discern what is important to you and what's just an unnecessary waste of time.

Maintain a Schedule

The importance of adhering to a set routine can't be overemphasized. Everyone, from the teen prepping for school to the head of the same college is required to adhere to a certain kind of routine. The world can appear as a tangled web without routine, and easy to be caught up in other things. Once you have decided your goals and achieve success first, the first step you should take is create a schedule for yourself. Be sure to set the time in to build your business and build relationships on the way. If you have the chance to peek into the lives of a extremely successful athlete or musician the first thing to look for is the frequency with which they follow an established routine.

Learn to Improve Your Skills

The world is rough, and competitors leave us with no choice but to improve our skills every second. You can't afford to miss every opportunity to enhance your capabilities. No matter what area you're in, you need to be aware that remaining active is the most effective method of making yourself more effective and profitable over the long haul. In reality, you don't glance around and there are plenty of skilled people who are ready to fill your shoes. What's the best way to make an efforts to not become outdated? What are you doing to add importance and at the exact at the same time be as tough or even stronger than all of your colleagues?

Whatever the circumstance is, be aware that enhancing yourself should be on your agenda. Don't be satisfied with the things you are able to do try to accomplish more, and strive to achieve it. Discover the skills that will enhance your career or help you develop at a personal level. Workshops, training degree, diplomas, and activities that can make you one step ahead of your peers is what you need to aim for to improve your skills. Be attentive and curious about the world around you, learn of the possibilities open to you on a personal basis which will help you grow both professionally and personally.

Learn about the market for jobs and supply chain and learn the skills that are needed most. For instance, you can learn a new language that is demanded on the global market. The goal is to become confident and competent enough to know what the demands of the moment are. You can take classes in French, Mandarin, and Spanish. There are many online courses for training and certificates available. Pick one that is pertinent to your needs and begin making progress on. You can study baking or pottery or cooking, and then learn any of those skills for a professional or in a way as a side venture. A side business that you incorporate could also result in additional funds to achieve your goals. Whatever the case when you are able to improve your skills and gaining experience, you'll always be in a win-win scenario. With more experience gained it will allow you improve your professional career to a higher level with a bright future.

Rise Every Time You Get Down

If you decide to embark on a path to reach your goal, you should be aware that failures are not unavoidable. Every time you win you will have the chance of a slip and fall. Most often than not, following a thorough dive, the climb isn't easy. If you take a look at the life of a lot of successful individuals around the globe you'll see that they all faced the possibility of failure at one time or another. The way they recovered from losing that was the key to their success. Walt Disney, for instance was told by a reporter from The Kansas City Star that he was not creative and had no an imagination that was strong. Did you know that he was dismissed from his job? Let's look at the way this failed performance helped his cause. He is now considered among the top innovative geniuses in the history of. Stories like these are an inspiration to those who are afraid of failure and is hesitant to try the new thing.

When you encounter an obstacle it's normal to feel down for a while. However, closing yourself up in your room and lamenting for days is not going to assist. However, this type of behaviour can stop you from achieving your goals and could be an obstruction in your progress. It's true that almost everyone is susceptible to sulking however, the time spent in negativity can be put to use to benefit other causes. Few successful people are known as the type of person who sulks.

The importance of professionalism can teach that you keep your personal and professional life separate. If things begin to merge there will be problems. The more organized you are when following your goals more easily you're likely to face. There will be numerous mistakes, and you'll be forced to pick yourself up again and do it again. Did you not see how many times sportsmen like Roger Federer, Lewis Hamilton as well as Cristiano Ronaldo have fallen short and have been criticized by fans across the globe? It is not acceptable to let their professional failures affect their confidence in themselves. If these extraordinary players chose to sit down and sulk in self-pity for long periods and then never back to their feet and provide an even better performance than they did the previous one. If the world comes to your rescue each time you're injured, you'll be at a distinct disadvantage. In the end you must always be aware of the importance of your goal and make sure you put forth all of your efforts until you reach your goal.

One thing you must remember is that you will not succeed unless you believe that you must always discover more. Every day is a chance to learn new things and getting rid of the outdated and dogmatic strategies you thought were superior. You can the necessary progress and begin getting closer to a place of satisfaction by putting your pride and ego aside. When you discover you are more detrimental to your progress more than other sins, you'll be shocked.

Chapter 3: Be Strategic

If you've decided to make a intention to achieve your goals an additional habit you must build is the capacity to develop effective strategies to achieve your goals. The ability to create an effective strategy is among the most essential qualities leaders must have. A plan for strategic execution is vital to achieve a goal since it gives an unambiguous sense of direction, with no chance of distracting.

Bill Gates, one of the most successful people in the world, has exhorted how important it was to put a solid plan in place. He stated that if the strategy isn't well-designed and effective, it will be unsuccessful, even if it is backed by reliable data. He also stated that an ineffective execution of a plan could cause harm or ruin the effectiveness of a strategy. It is a fact that when it comes to establishing an professional career, if there isn't an adequate preparation and a well-thought out plan, not is possible.

If we look at the basic instance of a company it is clear that there is no significant action undertaken without carefully planned planning. We've all heard the words'sales' and'market', and we've been concerned about these two terms. In particular, if there's any strategy that works for marketing and sales, these departments will be the ones to suffer most. Everyone who is successful in business will always be discussing the advantages of the plan. In the real world, no business will prosper without strategy.

What is the importance of strategy?

The past has revealed the crucial role of strategy. The past has numerous examples of the importance of strategic planning as part of the human civilization in general starting from invading countries and establishing societies creating governments, to organising coups.

People have been practising the art of strategizing for quite a while. It's an art form and a science form. Also, the process of completing simple tasks without planning can be challenging. Every problem can be dealt with easily if you employ an effective and clear strategy. You'll be able identify issues in marketing with some level of planning when you employ a smart strategies. Let's consider how vital strategy is in thriving in your life:

Strategy Gives Direction

Imagine that you are required to visit an acquaintance in a new place. You get in your car and drive after which you realize that you've been traveling around the same street every day. What would you think of yourself when you were faced with a scenario such as this? Most likely, you'd feel disillusioned and as being a failure, unable to even comprehend the obvious changes and twists that are the nature of the roads. It's similar to a feeling that a lot of people encounter at the same time in their lives: the feeling of feeling lost and lost and. One thing that can help in overcoming confusion is faith in a direction. Not just about the actual road, but the route to your success. You need confidence to develop the right decision.

The strategy you create must be crystal clear on the purpose of your strategy. It is important to know the main goal and what you'll do to follow the steps to reach your destination. It's also about developing habits that help you prepare for the future and help you prepare for any unexpected situations that may arise between now and then and. No matter the obstacles that you might confront, you must get up after each fall and go in the direction of your ultimate goal.

Most successful people don't employ a strategy that is not in the first place. Most people who have had success is meticulous enough to plan their actions depending on the circumstances. Strategies are a crucial factor in understanding each aspect of your journey to get the destination you wish to take in your life.

A perception of the direction you are heading is crucial. You've probably noticed that officials and government agencies that have the power to manage large numbers of citizens are always reviewing and revising their development strategies. There could be a myriad of reasons behind it, but the most important reason is to keep up with the rapid growth of modern times in order to ensure that things are working for the people of all ages. Even an individual as powerful and successful as the President has numerous strategies in the works, and different backup plans in the event that one of them fails should there be a massive emergency. So, it is clear the importance of focusing on a single goal for those who want to have a great chance of success in their lives.

In all honesty How will you grow in life if aren't trying to figure out the situation? You'll need to be persistent enough to keep moving towards your goal, without getting distracted by distractions. The plans you have in place must exist to assist you overcome any obstacles on the way. It is only possible to reach your goal with great success if adhere to the plan, and wisely!

Strategy can be helpful to Ensure Long Run

You've decided to take a step to achieve your goals Have you considered the strategies you can implement between the steps to be successful and be more successful? Numerous famous people took odd jobs in order to land opportunities in film industry or in the music industry. Stars such as Jennifer Aniston, Chris Pratt, James Franco, Rachel McAdams, and many others started out working in pubs and restaurants. Although they had plans to make it onto the big screen one day, their plan was to earn money until they got an enviable position in the entertainment industry. Justin Bieber also started as an Youtube celebrity and later became so popular that he was able to dominate the top charts of music. This means that you must have strategies to strike a bull's-eye on your main area of.

Most people who begin an exciting new venture has an immediate plan. It is essential to have short-term plans to be in place in the event that your plan fails. Strategizing is crucial to help you determine what you need to take action in any situation that could occur. Corporate and government industries, for instance, regularly create three- tofive-year plans based on their needs and project's scope. Planning is the way it prepares you to help you achieve your goals over the long term. Because of these strategies, you'll feel secure and at peace in your mind throughout the process. An organized strategy will give you confidence and desire to give the best you can in all that you undertake.

Strategies aid in getting feedback

Feedback is extremely important and isn't only about giving or getting scores. It is more effective to grow when a well-designed evaluation and feedback system has been in place. How do you imagine getting better if you don't acknowledge and accept your mistakes and shortcomings? There are a lot of large companies which have instituted reviews and feedback. If you look at it, you will find an evaluation system that is in place nearly everywhere.

If you are shopping at the mall, you'll see that they offer you the opportunity to fill in a questionnaire about their products and the way their staff treated you. Even a simple taxi ride can result in being evaluated as a customer and you will be able to grade your driver according to their professional conduct. This is considered to be an approach to determine the level of efficiency a procedure or person is doing and the extent to which advancement can be made in the areas that are of concern.

Feedback doesn't have to take the form of checklists which you use to mark off your experiences with the service you received. Chatting with someone you feel comfortable and at ease with could be an excellent way to discover numerous aspects that you might have missed in the end. Discussions that are open and honest will help you to understand diverse viewpoints. For instance, you could encounter a challenging situation working with a coworker but you might not be able approach the person at work in a professional or ethical manner. If you take the time to meet and discuss the issue with someone whom you trust, you might gain some insight into how to handle the troublesome colleague. A strategic approach is crucial when dealing with difficult people. If someone can help you identify the obstacles you've created to yourself, this may help in a variety of ways.

It is a lengthy process. It takes a lot effort and thoughtful ideas in order to progress and achieve success. People who are successful do not instantly achieve a status where they are constantly being praised. Every person goes through a period when they face criticism for their work or even for personal issues. Ego can be a significant obstacle in the path to success. You must be aware that when you get constructive criticism, you should keep it in perspective and examine the criticism to determine if it is true. aid in your improvement.

Plan your work and efforts to the point that you are open to taking other's views and suggestions. Be open to constructive criticism and make use of it to correct your weaknesses and shortcomings. Focus on areas in which you're lacking and put in the effort to meet your objectives. When you do this you will be able to use these assessments as a lesson and continue to work towards your goals by enhancing and correcting your errors at the same time. Make sure to record your progress and note the areas where you need to be corrected. In the end, you'll become polished in no time.

Strategy helps you prepare for the adversities that may come your way.

Adversities do not come into your life through knocking at the door. There aren't many who can say that they have never experienced any kind of hardship or setback throughout their lives. It's a fact there will be tough times regardless of how successful individuals on the planet. There will be occasions that, no matter how meticulously you plan your strategies there will be a mistake that you missed and, as a result you might be dealt an enormous blow. There are bound to be challenges, but no one can tell if a plan will succeed or not. One can use the scenario of investing in shares and stocks as an illustration. There will be times when the stock of a firm is in high demand which will increase in value. If there is a incident, all your capital invested in the business could be gone in a flash. It is impossible to predict the outcome of such a situation however, a plan to be prepared for the possibility of such challenges should be put in place.

It's important to realize this and can be a great way to learn also. If you've had a failure or loss in the past, it's likely that you'll be comfortable about the procedure and be better prepared for the next time. A strategic plan and backup plans are essential and must be practiced by all. The Covid-19 epidemic that spread across the globe killed a lot of people as well as ruined businesses and their livelihoods. Housekeepers, daily wage earners and private company employees performers, vendors, hotel workers, and many others have all experienced a severe setback. The global disaster has caused unimaginable suffering and nobody could have imagined that things could have turned out more dire. Nobody could have imagined that this kind of disaster could strike nearly every living thing at that speed of a scale. This tragedy proved that there is no way to predict the future and that nothing lasts forever.

It is recommended to have a backup plan in the event that your initial plan doesn't work. If you consider one specific instance of a hotel proprietor who suffered a substantial loss of money due to no revenue from tourism during the COVID-19 restrictions phases. Had they put a little of money for emergencies and not invested all their funds in buying the hotel they wouldn't be in the position of being bankrupt. Whatever your job or the method you earn money and resources, you must always set an effort to follow strategies to make savings. Money is a crucial factor in the lives of people and in large part it affects their peace of mind. Financial security is as one of the most effective methods of surviving any threat.

If you're thinking of embarking on a new project, business or other type of job, you should think carefully before rushing out. Make a plan, think through every aspect of the advantages and disadvantages of the situation. If you do this you'll be able to envision possible scenarios and make plans in case there are any issues that arise. So, it's important to create an action plan in case one plan doesn't work it will have another plan that will pick you up right where you were.

Strategy Is Profitable

Business professionals who are successful are always adamant about implementing strategies to maximize their profits in the long term. One can think of a famous business professional like Amazon's CEO Jeff Bezos, who always works with an approach that is strategic. For instance, in his letter to shareholders in 2016 it is clear that he has meticulously planned the goals he would like the company to achieve in the near future. As per the note the main fears is that the company may become less important and experience a slow decline. In the letter the author clearly outlines the methods that must be utilized to overcome situations such as this. His approach is based on the customer's obsession, taking on external perspectives, and avoiding intermediaries to help the company overcome difficult scenarios in the near future.

The pursuit of success is pursued by many. It would be impossible to even reach for one of those straws if there was no benefits to gain. Profit is what drives the world, and all the enterprises that are part of it. If you're trying to reach your goal of success, remember to establish a specific plan to achieve the maximum profit and success even in times when profits are difficult. Consider ways to improve your efficiency. An easy method of working smart, not only hard work, will help you get a lot of work done. Profit is vital to survive in this competitive and crowded world. Any small setback could be a major impact on the overall efficiency of your business. So, you must be savvy and devise strategies to make you very successful and make enormous profits from each business you set your sights on.

Strategic Communication

Without communication in its simplest form without the simplest of communication, there would not be a functioning world. Animals communicate with each other despite being able to communicate with each other despite the fact they don't communicate in a language, and this makes them stay bonded on the open field. Humans aren't any different. While we can speak in languages and don't have to rely on signals and gestures, being able to comprehend the thoughts of others can be a challenge at times.

There are many times you've heard someone mention "bridge between the two" as well as "communicate with somebody." If communication isn't in order and coordination, the functioning of any department could be extremely challenging. When it comes to connecting with those who can help you and your business achieve communicating is essential. Implementing a plan to understand the essentials to be successful within your industry is a great idea. It is possible to analyze your issue and work to make it better by implementing a well-designed communication strategy. If, for instance, you are in the field of marketing and wish to become an effective businessperson within short time you should be competent in implementing a successful marketing communications strategy.

Communication is crucial to developing relationships in your private life, and also to build professional relationships with customer and clients. Whatever the case the goal is to to articulate your viewpoint and ideas in a way that is clear front of people who need to know. If you don't communicate effectively, there will be the possibility of creating a number of misperceptions and misconceptions that could influence your future. A positive discussion and clear thoughts will allow you to succeed as an example. For instance, if you're an architect. Your client is looking to design his office the way he wants it. If both parties are clear on what they are looking for and exert a lot of effort to communicate their concepts, then it's unlikely the unity they have achieved fail. Communication, no matter the industry you are in, is vital to develop good relationships and network associations.

If you are prepared you will be able to tackle numerous unexpected problems immediately. Planning gives you a sense of direction and significantly increases effectiveness. This is the reason why big corporations and other companies often employ skilled individuals to manage a variety of projects. The practice of creating efficient plans prior to starting an undertaking, it can extremely beneficial over the long term. Begin by planning the day's schedule and then move on to bigger plans and more difficult goals. Your brain that you employ to develop a plan of action and then tackle one issue at a given time, could be extremely beneficial. Not only will having a clearly defined method and action program assist to overcome difficulties and obstacles, but it could assist you in running your business successfully. You can develop a strategy to achieve the primary goal of your plan however, it won't be accomplished in a short time. Any strategy that works efficiently requires a plan as well as numerous other backup plans. So, the more emphasis is placed on the importance in being organized, the better it's going to be. Develop strategies, and great ones, but be professional and pursue your goals with a methodical approach.

In the end that it does not matter how high you're in the climb to success. The most important thing is the way you formulate your plans and then how you implement them into action every day as a professional and a personal one. It's extremely difficult to succeed without a well-thought-out strategy. If you're a professional or someone who is looking to reach the same level of success as the people you admire have, then you must adopt a strategic approach. This is the kind of the planning that will allow you to take action and persevere in a specific manner to accomplish your goal.

Chapter 4: Be Flexible

The well-known billionaire, Mukesh Ambani, is an entrepreneur, and is often known as the face of modern Indian industrialist. In fact Mukesh Ambani is the chairperson of Reliance Industries, a Fortune 500 Company as well as is the owner of numerous other business companies and brands. He is considered to be as one among the top-performing individuals across the globe. When he made one of his remarks in which he stressed not to give up, and to try again and again, since becoming successful the first time isn't always feasible.

If successful individuals who are of a high standing speak about something similar to this, you can take it as a learning experience. There are no two people around the world are alike, they might be alike, but they will possess one or two traits that make them different. Uniqueness is a great quality. However, you shouldn't benefit from this trait but rather be able to absorb the different perspectives of various people.

Why do we need flexibility?

Permanence is a broad concept and has many meanings. There is no way to say that everything is considered to be eternal and that includes us, whom claim to be the best beings over the other creatures. From the beginning of time to the present the world has witnessed massive transformations. The saying goes that changing is the only thing that will never change. What's the most effective way to learn to help yourself get through the ever-changing times? The answer is in one word, and that word is flexibility!

The ability in adapting to a changing scenario, regardless of how challenging it is will determine your strengths. The strength you have can give you a an advantage in your quest for success. Use it as your testing period. If you put in the effort to adapt to changes and new methods as you notice how positive things begin to improve. In the end, it's your attitude and your mental attitude that will allow you to beat even the most challenging of circumstances. A lot of great leaders, especially those in the business world, are known for their capacity to adapt. The constantly changing market trends and the variety of tastes of customers can cause a variety of problems when taking care of every tiny aspect that gets in the path to victory.

Another example could be the case when you've been employed at a business for several years and you have landed one of the top jobs in the company. You encounter a group of fresh employees who are vibrant and young They are different in their approach to various aspects of their work. Instead of being upset and being swayed by your own ego, all could you do instead is to listen to their ideas and opinions and determine whether they're valuable. It is crucial to be open to new ideas and open to different ways of thinking. That's how you can take an open mind. A different person's ideas might not be the most effective solution however it can help keep you on the right track and help you in changing your thinking to a better one.

But, a flexible approach to life isn't easy. It's a skill that must be developed gradually and with lots of effort. Think about the following reasons as to why being flexible is an attribute and a trait that everyone must have to achieve great success:

Expectations Can Be Disappointing

There are likely to be times in your life when you desired something from a loved one, a colleague or even your acquaintances, and have received the exact opposite. It's not wrong to assert that there are times in one's life which are filled with disappointments , and things will not seem to go according to plan.

The year of 2019, for example, has established records for itself as an extremely difficult and difficult years for many people from all over the world due to the outbreak of COVID-19. In the final quarter of 2019 there was a report that a virus dubbed COVID-19 was beginning to cause havoc across areas of China. We had no idea the possibility of it spreading this rapidly, and at the end of 2020 the virus would have infected almost every nation on earth. This is a great example of the way that next few years could be uncertain. Didn't everyone have plans? Yes however, we were all kept inside our houses for months at a stretch Many people suffered the loss of their life, families, their friends, or career as a result! Every plan we created were put in limbo.

Think about this in the following how: in the near future, many scenarios might arise which are far beyond the imagination of you. What is the routine that you follow to assist you through this kind of situation? It's your flexibility! If you're stuck in a rigid view and a lack of willingness to change your perspective to the changing circumstances that change, you'll face numerous challenges to achieving success in life. The frustration that comes due to the failure of a plan could be a challenge enough. But, it's your ability to adapt that helps you to be open to the perspectives of different people and keep your current and prepared for the future.

An attitude that is flexible can be an advantage

Attitude can allow you to win the situation, and it could cause more trouble for the other person. You should be aware that not all circumstances in life will go according to the original plans. There will be challenges and disappointments. Your attitude is crucial; it is what gives the peace you need for the long-term and bring positive and helpful people to your life. There have been many instances that have involved the tone of your voice played a significant impact in resolving issues and, often it has led to more conflicts. Your ability to adapt can allow you to overcome a lot of the difficulties you face. Dissociating yourself from your pride and thinking from another perspective is an extremely productive step on your behalf. The less conflicts you're engaged in the higher your chances of living an easy life. Flexibility will allow you to see things more clearly and have more perspective. This means you'll always be ahead in any challenging circumstance. This not only provides you with an optimistic outlook, but also a possibility to have your final decision, which can be essential in any circumstance.

Think about a situation in which you couldn't be able to attend your graduation because your friend was injured in an accident, and you had to get him to the emergency department instead. You'd be angry about being denied a once-in-a lifetime occasion to be able to be a part of your graduation celebration. But, it is dependent on your perspective. Imagine what could be the outcome if you had not sent your friend straight into the medical facility. It's likely that the person would have suffered an injury that could affect his health throughout his life. But, you had to make the decision to choose between your friend's life and the priceless wedding you'd like to be a part of.

Similar to that, there will come occasions in your life when you will have to choose between two choices. There are many occasions where you be unable to take advantage of great opportunities, but it's your responsibility to understand that a setback doesn't necessarily mean you must bury your head in self-pity. Be flexible and be positive when they occur.

Problem Finding Attitude

Just hearing about a situation can make an otherwise bright day look bleak. It's very challenging to see a smile in the face of bleak situations, but you'll observe that on a lot of occasions, people attempt to maintain positive attitudes. Everyone is not a fan of challenges and is likely to do to stay clear of any circumstance that might get them in difficulty.

A person who glows with a creative mindset is what people love the most. It isn't easy to attain. A long-term commitment and a shrewd approach are required to get to the position that helps you guide your career in an upward direction. If you're a person that makes you regret every little bump in your path, achieving your goals could seem like a distant idea. Troubles are often associated with difficulties, and it's an accepted fact that they will occur in one's professional or personal life. You've probably noticed within your family that people in your family take every circumstance with no remorse and others may create more anxiety at the sight of one problem. What does it make people more flexible when it comes to every issue? There is a possibility that certain individuals are more powerful than others. This obviously is debateable. But, you can't ignore the fact that effort is one of the most important components that can help people achieve their goals.

Imagine that you are the head of a business that has a lot of employees working on your projects. As well as all the others, if you can find someone who is eager to assist others and is able to solve problems with a positive attitude You should pay particular attention to this person. Everyone would like to surround themselves with people who have a positive attitude and isn't easily affected by challenges. Everyone doesn't want to be around someone who is depressed and weak because of small incidents. A negative attitude could affect the mood of any space, which could cause serious problems in the present as well as in the future. It is important to realize that complaining won't solve any issue. Only a positive attitude that promotes the effort to solve the issue can make you succeed in your life.

Your attitude towards every adversity will help you overcome the most difficult of challenges in your life. Each problem must have a solution. And when there's no solution it is possible to discuss ideas with others who could help solve the issue.

Get caught up on what you've Not Known About

The generation of millennials has come up with a number of lingos. One that you might have heard of is "FOMO," that stands for "fear of being left out." In the event that you take a second to think about it you might find an important significance to this uber-trendy term. The challenges of life can appear in many forms, some can bring immense happiness while others can bring suffering. But, in the middle of instances is a space where a variety of emotions are constantly nurtured. Humans are so immersed in their jobs and other aspects of their lives that they frequently do not notice various happenings and circumstances that could have been beneficial to them.

There will be occasions that you'll do something that you feel a bit tense, for instance, if you decide to take a trip that you don't feel enthusiastic about with your buddies. If you choose to approach the trip with a positive mindset you could find it as one of the most memorable experiences you've had during your entire life. There will be a lot of instances when your plans will not match with what actually takes place. In situations like such that you need to be prepared to be flexible when it comes to your strategy. Flexibility will assist you in handling unexpected situations. There are numerous stories of how famous and successful individuals got the positions they held. Marilyn Munroe was indeed a world-renowned star However, did you realize that she was initially rejected by her initial agency? The agency advised her that she needed to get an administrative job, and she was not able to have the capacity to be an entertainer of any kind. Check out how she changed the rules and became one of the most popular celebrities.

The seasons change and the things change, too. There will be times in your life where you feel like you're not in control of certain aspects of your life. Certain things, whether either way, can never change, no regardless of what you do. When you begin a new project, you have big expectations however, as the weeks progress, you'll realize that things don't meet your expectations and thoughts. There will be times when you aren't happy with the things you've achieved thus far. After some careful thought you might be compelled to change the plans and instructions.

It's perfectly normal and totally normal to be overwhelmed and dissatisfied in your job. It's a good idea to consider your goals and what you do not wish to do. It is your only chance to pull you out of any stressful situation that's not helping you. An inflexible personality and an unflexible mind will not only cause more problems but also create more problems. Your dreams are yours only and you should not feel accountable for anything except yourself. So rather than doing something to impress someone else in your life, choose to do things that make you feel happy.

It's not a problem to change your perspective and working towards something completely different or a profession completely. The priorities you set can change as time passes, and items that were once considered to be the most important thing in your life may now be put aside to focus on something that is more essential. Make sure you are certain about the things you think is most important for you. Pause between various priorities to comprehend and modify what you've chosen to do. Then return to your journey in the same way as if you'd not halted your plans.

If you're ever feeling down or regrettable about a choice consider a look at your surroundings and consider how many successful individuals have switched careers and gone into becoming some of the most successful individuals on the planet. There is no age too old to embark on the next chapter and pursuing a career path later in life is also a great idea. It is important to continue moving forward with an objective in life which keeps you satisfied and focused throughout. In this kind of situation keeping a positive outlook and being flexible will allow you to sail through even the most difficult storms.

Your position or title can never protect you from the challenges that could be faced in your daily life. It's not a wise idea to become too fixated about your perspective. You need to be able to change. You're probably thinking of ways you can improve your ability to adapt considering how difficult it is. The answer lies in you! Your viewpoint should be rational and free of personal conceits. Once you've removed yourself from what other people might think of you can you achieve what you believe to be correct with total conviction and clarity. Thus, you must come to terms with your strengths and weaknesses and get yourself ready for the possibility of facing any challenge with confidence and determination.

Chapter 5: Unplug From Distractions

Our modern lifestyle has us with the access to gadgets and technology that keep us entertained for a considerable amount of time. You might want to get your favorite book and stay sitting on the couch reading it, but you'll also find yourself looking into your mobile phone every occasionally. This is exactly the way distractions appear and feel like. This is a straightforward example of how even a small interruption can distract you and stop you from achieving your objectives.

It's also common to be distracted by other things as you do your job. The problem arises when these distractions begin to become an obstacle in your life. It is important to recognize the issues that cause you to fall in comparison to everything else, and transforming your goals to a distant goal.

In most cases when people find themselves in difficult circumstances the potential of their character is recognized. Have you heard the tale of how the famous and enchanting characters Harry Potter came into being? Most people aren't aware of J.K. Rowling, who created the fantastic world of magic in her novel Harry Potter and the Philosopher's Stone. In numerous instances she has spoken about how being through a crisis in her finances forced her to turn to her writing. She wrote the first novel from Harry Potter. Harry Potter series while attending her child in a café.

J.K. Rowling was a single mother as well as her professional and personal lives were completely off balance. She was rejected by 12 publishers but she did not give up. In her determination to accomplish something extraordinary in life, and to protect her family as well as herself from being a burden She wrote her book and kept all distractions in check regardless of how hard they proved to be. She's shown how you can rise above extreme situations if determined and gifted enough, and keep working to improve and sharpen their abilities.

There are other poets and writers who have found themselves in quiet places to focus on their work in complete silence. The reason that artists choose to remain in a secluded area is to keep distractions from hindering their ability to think. The more isolated one remains, the more concentrated they are believed to be. Artists, and many other artistic people, employ this strategy of being secluded from the noises of the daily world in order to get their work completed.

The more focused and concentration, the better your ability to produce impressive results. Distractions can be dangerous to anyone who is working on business. However, it's the way you handle such a circumstances that determines your strengths. Many people cannot afford to isolate themselves for the greatest results However, what anyone can do is adjust to the situation and improve their concentration so that they reap rewards, even in the most difficult of circumstances. Knowing what distractions can affect your most will aid in avoiding the elements that can distract you. Becoming aware of distractions will allow you to achieve your goals with minimal delay.

What are the reasons distractions can be harmful?

In today's multitasking world that is thriving, many are working all day and night to make a living and to achieve where they would like to be. The distractions can certainly occupy your life and mind every often. It could be in the form of family, friends, food, drinks, books as well as the internet or even something as basic as a television program. It's difficult to know for sure which distractions are harmful to you , but if you're having fun there is a good chance that you'll discover all of it correct.

If simple tasks turn into serious habits, distractions could turn into a risk. For instance, you could have a two-day deadline on your project however, you're so caught up in watching the latest episode of your favorite show that you delay the work. Stress of putting things off until late can lead to poor outcomes. This kind of behavior is likely to compromise the quality of your work as well as your credibility. In the end it's essential to disconnect from all distractions, no regardless of how small you may be, and concentrate on achieving your goals and achieving success.

Be able to overcome distractions

A step back from the things that weigh your down is one of the most positive choices you'll take. What you have to get rid of is things that may become obstacles on your way to success. It is crucial to determine what the nitty-gritty divergences in your life which are hindering your progress from being fully realized with one goal.

Let's discuss some possible ways that you can avoid distractions:

Recognize Your Bad Habits

Habits can take time to establish themselves in the routine of a person and may be developed through experience or from repeating the same behavior over a lengthy time. Recognizing and overcoming your negative habits is vital in advancing your personal development and professionally. Once you've identified your pattern of when and where you're most distracting, it's easier to stay clear of these situations. It is said that you'll never acquire a good sense of practices. Be aware of the actions you're taking and whether your actions could be damaging the prospects of your business.

There are times when you have missed a particular habit of yours until someone mentions it to you. It's easy to slip into defensive mode and refuse to believe that it is true however, if you look back and examine your behavior and habits, you'll realize there are some habits of yours which could be a source of irritation for many and, more importantly could be the reason you've been struggling recently. So, it is essential to know what behaviors are beneficial and what ones can be detrimental to your success and growth. Be sure to put aside your ego as well as denial , and take the reviews you receive from your peers and then examine the facts and then follow the recommendations to set your goals high, so that no bad behavior can be a hindrance to your success. It is your responsibility to teach the best methods into your daily routine at work. Be sure you're in the right direction and strive to achieve your goals by implementing all the necessary actions to achieve success in your life.

Do every positive thing to get closer to your goal. Plan your schedule so that you know exactly what you'd like. Keep away from lengthy TV shows and quit having a drink as often; remain focused and constantly look for ways you can improve yourself. Keep your thoughts in check and never let the slightest distraction penetrate your mind. Be aware that it's you and your unwavering effort that will get you to places. One thing to be aware of is that nearly everyone who is successful has made sacrifices to achieve the level at which they are. So, any behaviour that could be getting against your dreams must eliminate right away.

Set Daily Goals

The goals you have set may be an ambitious goal for the future however, to realize them, you have to be focused enough to focus on each day. Setting goals for your day is the best method to boost your productivity. It's likely that you've noticed that putting off work or putting off tasks until tomorrow feels great at the time But what happens when work gets overwhelming and creates anxiety?

According to what Jack Welch said, you need to change your behaviour before the circumstances make you alter your behavior. If you're working towards long-term goals it's easy to be caught in the middle, and confused on what you need to do on a regular basis. This is the purpose of daily planning. It's as important to maintain a regular regimen as to maintain an excellent mind. A lack of focus even for just a single day, can create psychological turmoil and cause a huge negative. You might have a lengthy list of tasks to complete in order to reach your goal If you don't begin to check each day off the list and you don't, you'll be left with a long task list at the end of the day.

It is crucial to be able to articulate a clear idea of what you would like to achieve and the best way to achieve it. You must be aware of the methods you employ and set daily goals that assist you in improving your performance both personally as well as professionally. The gift of time is given to us by the human race and it's our responsibility for us to get the best of it. One of the most resented practices that successful people will talk about is time waster. Start by establishing the habit of creating daily schedules and goals. The moment you get up you should open your journal and write down your three goals each day. The sooner you begin making progress towards your goals, the quicker you'll be able to accomplish every goal. The rewards aren't just about achieving objectives, but rather the feeling of satisfaction that you get after working according to your daily schedule. The idea of not wasting the day's work time to unnecessary tasks can lead to the highest amount of motivation. After one day of accomplishment and you'll soon be in the habit of experiencing this feeling again.

Start by setting three goals for each day that you must achieve, slowly increasing the amount of tasks you have to complete. It might be a single day at a stretch, but you'll see that this practice will allow you to reduce your workload and stress that you typically face at the end of the day. It's a great routine that can prepare you for the next day as well as while giving you the space to review or edit the work you've accomplished over the last few days.

If a project needs for completion, the majority of people would expect it to be finished within a couple of days. This can be a problem as the job may be affected as a result. By dividing your work responsibilities and finishing them in a reasonable amount of time may give you the opportunity to reflect on your own performance and also allow you to enhance your abilities. After a few weeks you'll find that this great routine has become automatic to you and you'll have the ability to be productive each day.

Clear You Mind

Decluttering is always beneficial in any way, whether it's cleaning out your house and taking away all your trash or clearing your mind and getting rid of any negative thoughts. Cleaning is a positive word that can bring numerous advantages for someone who is determined to make a difference in their life. Your mind is the only thing you have to influence your actions. As you care for your body by feeding it adequate nutrition and proper exercise Your mind must be fed by positivity and clarity of thought. A cluttered mind can cause confusion and lead to a confused mind. This can be a disaster for anyone but especially for someone who is looking to be successful.

It is important to have quiet in order to achieve an inner peace and body. The hustle and the constant competition makes our lives full of noise. These issues often reflect in your mind when you try to relax at night, however, the thoughts of your day remain in your head. Remember the moment you were the last time you felt happy and content. Utilize that as an inspiration and try to solve any issues that could be causing you stress. Be sure to get rid of the numerous stressors that can distract the mind often. Look for the things that cause an effect on you or more precisely, cause your emotions to rise. When you've figured out what triggers your emotions you feel and think about certain events in your life, you'll be able to confident that your thoughts will be clear of the clutter and baggage that has been bothering you for a long time.

Cleaning your thoughts is an important aspect of clarity by focusing your mind on what you would like to achieve for yourself. For instance, if you are a guest for a lengthy time at a party and you interact with a large number of people, it is likely that you will recall discussions you shared with a handful of them for several days. Whatever you try, the atmosphere created by the gathering will remain in your mind and occupy your mind for a long period of time. There is a chance that you're not losing focus on your thoughts, but in some way, you're influenced by thoughts of specific people or gatherings, and then you begin to drift off. Your mind will keep racing until you can stop it from doing this. It's a vicious cycle of distracting yourself.

If you notice that you're too consumed with certain thoughts and feelings You know it's time to get rid of your thoughts. Be sure to look over your surroundings and determine the things that are the source of your thoughts. If you're unable to solve all the thoughts that are ringing in your head, you should take a break. Relax while letting your thoughts rest for a few minutes. The many voice messages, phone calls texts as well as social media platforms news, and television can all be like a form filled with noise in your brain. You could also begin to practice some types of yoga that are believed to reduce the mind wandering problems. So, it's important to take a deep breath and have a few days or two, and return with a clear and focused mind to get back to work with a great enthusiasm.

Prioritize Quality over Quantity

If you've been in an office with a closed-off area and you've had the experience of some coworkers who be late for work after their shift had ended. Some do this due to their inefficiency and need more time to complete their work, while others do it due to having lots of work to do and spend more hours at work to appear to their bosses and keep their admiration. The volume of work involved can exhaust you. But, one thing you should always keep in mind is that whichever strategies you pick for rat racing it is the work you put into your efforts that will create the most impact.

According to the Parkinson's law, the longer we allow ourselves to accomplish an activity, the more time it will take.. The reason for this is that our brains function in a way that, if we think that we have time we feel a bit more relaxed when it comes to completing our work on time. A successful person will never recommend taking longer to finish something that could have been accomplished at the same standard in just a few hours.

Set a time limit that you can focus on and finish your work. With shorter timeframes will allow you to concentrate on the work to be completed and produce work faster. While at work, you should take smaller coffee or smoke breaks. The time you take could be better used to get more work completed during the day. Always be a person who is open and eager to know more.

Every person you meet has a story to tell and a story to tell. Be sure to never undervalue anyone else's accomplishments, instead take a lesson from their experiences. It is not necessary to learn from your elders and teachers. You might not be aware in time and yet, you could learn a lot from people you believe aren't really relevant. The challenges that every person faces can be an excellent lesson on which they will not be only an educator, but also what needs to be done to achieve success. The quality of work you perform and the kind of person you are in the course of achieving the things you desire in life are crucial to your success. It is your mindset and ability to keep a positive impression on those who might assist you in your professional career.

If you are given more time, you're most likely to slow your pace and get distracted during the pauses. These distractions can help you feel relaxed However, they also have the ability to distract you and hinder your ability to achieve your goal.

Arrange Your Workspace

Ambiance and the energy in your surroundings can affect how you feel and act. This is different for different individuals. There are geniuses who are believed to be messy and claim to perform their best in messy spaces. The space you spend the majority of your time in is your home away from home, and it should be more relaxing. The first step you can do to organize your workspace is to know exactly what type of workspace will suit your needs the most. Perhaps you have an obsessional cleaning problem and would like every piece of furniture in the exact spot it needs to be. There is also the person who is greatly invigorated and inspired by just one image of a person who is successful hanging on the wall. It's like going back to your school days, when you were arranging your bedroom, as well as your study table, based on your personal preferences and tastes.

It is important to have a routine however, having the perfect workplace environment can work wonders to get the best outcomes. It's not everyone's dream of a home in the woods when they wish to write. What they can do is create a space which improves their state mind to aid the writer in reaching their goal. The method that follows could be extremely efficient.

In an interview from 2004, Haruki Murakami, a famous Japanese writer, talked about how he manages his writing with his lifestyle. He also said that when he starts writing a novel the writing begins in the early hours of four a.m. and writes for between five and six hours in a row. He has an exercise routine which includes a 10-kilometer run which is followed by a 1500-meter swimming. He reads, or listens to his favorite music prior to going to bed around 9 p.m. He explained that this routine is what keeps him captivated and helps keep him in a relaxed mental state.

If you're facing an arduous situation that can make you think about your capabilities and focus Make sure that you create an environment that assists you in accomplishing the task with greater efficiency. Be sure to stay away from all distractions, and everything that can make you feel attracted to them. Make fewer breaks and devote an appropriate period of time to work. Make sure your workspace is tidy and you aren't tempted to become distracted.

If you're seeking success, remember that sacrificing a long-term objective to satisfy your desires for the moment could cause a number of back-slides. If you're committed to being the person you wish to be, and reaching the goals you have set for yourself, you must be committed to a hard-working lifestyle without any distractions to keep you off track. The simple strategies outlined above will assist you in keeping your eyes off any distractions on the way.

Distractions can actually can be hazardous and result in more harm than you would think. If it comes to something that is crucial you've probably noticed even a momentary distracting yourself can make you lose concentration on the task in the moment. It's important to keep in mind that by putting the strategies for overcoming distracting factors into action, you will be able to get all those results faster and more easily.

Chapter 6: Think And Wait

Many of Leonardo's fans were thrilled when he received an Oscar for his The Revenant film The Revenant in the year 2016. The moment was so enthralling that all of his failures in the past to win deserved awards appeared to matter anymore. If you take it in the context of a long-term perspective, there's much to learn about his success after winning an Oscar.

Dicaprio was considered for nominations to an Academy Award six times before receiving one. Many of his fans and film critics believed the actor should have been awarded at other times too, and believed that he earned the award much.

The excitement that was observed all over the world through various online platforms for social networking was an incredible experience by itself. If you look at Dicaprio's professional chart, you'll see how many films he needed to be involved in and the many characters he was required to play over the course of his career. He didn't win an Oscar in a flash It was a long process of dedication and, more importantly, massive amounts of perseverance on his part to get to that he is at. Prioritizing your goals is vital in establishing a high degree of perseverance, since there will never be any obstacle to stop you from reaching your objectives. In order to be successful in life, you need to always be prepared to face many setbacks. However, it's how you climb back up and continue your journey with incredible determination that will help you get through any challenge. Each time you fall, think and sit, then move on with confidence.

Why is Patience the Key to success?

The success stories of the majority of people you have met would inform that it's not possible to achieve in one shot. The amount of effort and sweat that is required to reach the top spot is undisputed. It is true that life can be unfair at times You may find yourself in a variety of situations in which you think you've gained more than a family member or a sibling but were still given a lavish reward. You'll feel disappointed often due to faulty opinions and work-related politics.

There will be many occasions when you anticipate an immediate change of things. The fact that you have commit your mind and body in the project doesn't ensure that you'll be rewarded or even admired by your superiors or bosses. The way life is played is similar to an athletic game and you'll have to overcome all the obstacles and overcome all obstacles along the way. And but, when the game gets to the point of an objective, the player who is the most successful takes the lead. This is intriguing because, regardless of how long it takes you to reach what you want, if have always been adamant and dedicated to your goal, the odds are good that you'll receive what you deserve regardless of what the circumstance. But, it will require enormous thinking and patience. To succeed, you'll have to be patient for more than you could ever imagine.

How you handle the process of failure and success is a behavior you should build within yourself. If you are attentive to everything and try to get results in a hurry however, the satisfaction and quality you get from this success may not be satisfactory. The ability to be patient could appear to be an easy skill to acquire but it is difficult to implement. There are some steps you could follow to develop patience and achieve success:

A Long-Term Approach to Success

If you've watched The Defiant Ones, a documentary about two most popular performers in the world of music, Dr. Dre and Jimmy Iovine, then you've seen that success doesn't arrive to you with a silver spoon It is earned through many years of dedication and dedication. It's a fact that success can be attractive and many will take any step to attain it in a short amount of time.

Of course, if you observe signs of nepotism in your work area it is easy to believe there may be ways to succeed for the most powerful individuals around. The fact that this is the case can diminish your motivation; instead, you should strive for getting to a certain level with your own determination and efforts rather than relying on someone else's suggestion or favor. The satisfaction you get from working long and hard to achieve your goals is the most satisfying feeling you can ever experience. It's not only about achieving your target, but rather how you get there that will make you an accomplished person at the beginning.

Many have reached the top and been able to share their achievements to the world. No one of them would endorse a plan of shortcut to get to their goal. You'll be inspired discover more the story of Oprah Winfrey and her achievements in her life. She was the victim of abuse as a young child and the consequences was more extensive than what an individual child can endure. After many years of struggle and the successes that was achieved she has made a bigger contribution to society, aiding in the passage of 1994's U.S. National Child Protection Act that was which was signed in the name of President Clinton. She is an inspirational role model and example for those who believe in perseverance and perseverance. She is a shining example of how achievement that is achieved through perseverance can bring rewards that go beyond amount. There were no shortcuts for her and she certainly worked to the max to achieve a goal she was determined to achieve. It is a fact that there is no success without exertion. It is essential to put in a substantial amount of effort and time to accomplish your goals. Never give up an alternative regardless of how long it takes. with perseverance, you should also realize that there isn't a way to achieve success.

Career Benefits

If you're a proponent of being patient even in tough situations, it can be an advantage in numerous ways. The benefits of patience in your profession will aid in achieving great outcomes. If you are aspiring to professional success, you'll encounter numerous challenges that challenge your assumptions as well as test your morals and challenge your inner power. In this kind of situation just a bit of perseverance will allow you to climb each time.

If you're in a stressful situation the patience you have will grant you the ability to think, think, wait and then react appropriately. The word "patience" doesn't mean you have to deal with the trauma or abuse of your loved ones, and you believe as if the person have a change of heart and all would be okay and all would be well. It is the mindset that is put into patience and increases its value.

There are chances that you have made choices in the past, and regretted some of them. Humans have a tendency to be impulsive and regret it later. If it's your professional career that is affected, it could create a huge problem in the near future. If you manage your job, and you have a list of goals and an objective to get to, you have to be extra careful and behave in a manner that is shrewd and thoughtful. If you are lucky that your colleagues or your superiors realize that you're not the least patient when it comes to situations that could cause major harm to your progress in the business.

Human judgment is an issue for those who suffer as work ethics and politics are often a battle in the closed-doors of many companies. In this scenario it's difficult to engage in even the slightest act which could be considered non-professional at all. It is virtually impossible to be wrong in the process of thinking and taking the time to create an enduring foundation for yourself. So the more you allow yourself the time to think before you act and deciding what to do, the more likely you are to be on the right path to success.

Boosts Upskilling

People are always looking to improve their living in terms of living and conditions. However, the booming growth of different industries and sectors of work have created an environment of work that is the highest regard for effort and the acquisition of additional abilities. If you are willing to take some time to look through the recruitment section of various firms, anyone may be surprised by the wide range of abilities required on the job market. In fact, some of the abilities sound like the fake alien language called "Klingon"! In this massive rise of competition, how can you allow you to survive? It's simple that you are forced other than to improve your skills frequently. The amount of patience needed to learn and then unlearn in every stage of your career may be difficult to handle. But, with a little perseverance, you can be calm and take advantage of every chance that you get to further develop your profession.

The endurance required in a time of patience may impact your growth and help you achieve success. It is, for instance, your responsibility to determine the reason you're in an environment that doesn't meet your needs. Did you not get the opportunity to work or get a job due to not having the essential qualifications or you just left out? If you examine the circumstances and discover that you don't have the necessary skills to progress the right way, it's your character of persistence and patience that must be the main focus. Learn your pattern, comprehend the reasons you aren't capable of completing an assignment or task.

The next step is for you to put in efforts to upgrade your skills to be able to advance your career in the near future. It is important to note that learning to upgrade your skills takes patience and time as well as a lot of patience. If you are thinking and believe you require an additional training or degree to enhance your list of qualifications, start now to begin. Learn more about research, ask your teachers and colleagues on what they've been up to in order to remain relevant. And If you don't receive answers directly from them, don't fret, just browse the web and find out what you can do to improve your professional career. There's plenty of information available in the event you take a look. Be patient as you go through looking through information and figuring out the most important steps you require to follow for your strategy. As time passes, you'll become so proficient in practicing persistence that you'll experience nothing difficult in waiting and waiting for the perfect moment to conclude your agreement. The most important thing is to be committed for success, and it is this mindset that will help you to develop further skills in your quest for ultimate success.

Boosts Networking

A frequently talked about strategies used by successful people is networking and making connections. If you are employed by an organization, the federal government business or even your own business the one thing you must be aware of is the need to communicate. You've probably observed by now the way your interactions or interactions with certain people at work could affect your business.

Relations between people can be complex and difficult to handle for a majority times. Being a solo worker could be a nightmare for many. If you are working with others who are different, you must act as a peer, colleague or mentor, boss as well as many other things. But it's how you interact with others that will determines the final outcome. The truth is that dealing with people requires patience on a different degree. It takes time, effort and energy normally required to grasp the perspectives and opinions of different individuals can be a daunting task. It is not always possible for everyone to come with the same perspective as youdo; it's your determination within you that keeps your professional and assist you in reaching your goals quickly.

It is a good example of the music and film industry. The majority of directors and film makers work with the same group of people they have worked with prior or worked with for a long period of time. In order for actors to get parts on big screens as well as the TV, they need to be more effective in networking and interacting with people relevant to their work. Interactions play an important part in the process of making a decision. For instance, if you are working on a project that needs to be completed and need an additional pair of hands to help the first step you should do is consult your closest friends, those you trust to suggest the person who is the best person for that job. The chain operates in a manner that the person who is giving you the suggestion will mention the name of someone they've had contact with, or seen a lot of recently. So, it is clear how this loop of network is working. It's not only for the case in show business. This chain is equally effective in other fields.

Believing that you are in a slump is not your option. You must be able to recognize that there are specific ways of working that various companies and organizations operate. It is possible that you do not enjoy the atmosphere of a company which is why, in such a circumstance, it is important to consider the things you don't like about it consider making an overall list of pros and cons and identify exactly the issues you are experiencing. It can be a challenging circumstance to alter the culture and may take time to alter different attitudes and attitudes, but it's up to you to choose which one you would like to be an integral part of, and which you'd like to get rid of.

The key point to note is that just because success is not attained early, it doesn't mean that you're not able to achieve. It can take years of learning and relearning to achieve a level of success that you believe to be the most rewarding. So, the one important thing to remember is that success isn't easily achieved. Doubt and taking rash decisions without thinking about them could cause more harm than you ever thought. Make sure you keep your cool, and keep going forward to get what you've always wanted. The ability to persevere is definitely an important but it's not the only factor in success.

Chapter 7: The Most Important Asset Is You

Sir Edmund Hillary and Tenzing Sherpa were the two first to climb Mount Everest in the year 1953. Hillary was an explorationist as well as an avid mountaineer. He once stated that it's not about conquering mountains or summits, but, at the end of the day it's about taking on ourselves. This quote is crucial in developing confidence and motivation those who want to achieve success in life.

It is important to recognize your position as "the advantage," no matter what you do in your life. There may be instances where you've been unsure and lost in the demands of your work and personal life. If you are in the rat race present, it's evident that you'll tend to be a bit confused and be self-conscious and over-relying on other people. But, when you're in the process to achieve the success you've always dreamed of be sure to look after yourself as your most valuable asset. If you fail to take care to keep yourself safe and secure the ultimate ambitions could be lost in the end. It is not worth getting any results when you're not well-nourished mentally or physically.

The majority of the time we think to be the sole person we've ever known personally is ourselves. But, if you think upon a period that you were a bit unsure about what you were looking for and why you chose it, you'll realize that there could be multiple layers of thoughts in your head that make you feel confused about who you really are and what you're hoping to accomplish in your life.

Be confident in yourself

There is a long-standing law that gives a lot of importance to the concept of attraction. The law is based on the basis of being so convinced of something that you can make it happen by yourself. Also, if you've got an attitude of trusting in yourself you can increase your confidence to a point which will allow you to achieve your goals! It can be difficult to deal with situations and often you will not achieve the results you would like. However, that doesn't mean you are not capable of achieving more in your life. No matter if you're an 18-year old or 60 It doesn't matter when you begin planning and working towards your final goal. If you've got a strong faith in yourself and in your abilities, this will enable you to continue on the direction you want to go.

The confidence you have in yourself is what allows you to push forward with determination and determination. An even a tiny doubt could shake the confidence you have in your abilities and accomplishments. Building confidence at the start is the most effective way of knowing that you are an important asset. You are the most valuable thing in the world and you're the only one who can guide you to the goal you want and other factors can help you along the way. No matter how huge your ambitions are, it's how fervently you go after them that will determine the success you have achieved. Here are some simple ways to incorporate into your daily routine which will help you become more confident and will help you believe in yourself

We've already talked about in previous chapters how important the clarity of your thinking can be. True the opposite of being opinionated, and on the "right path" are two distinct instances. If you want to succeed in life, you have to first realize that keeping all of your opposing views in check, and that your thoughts could be wrong also. Breathe deeply and then think of the thoughts that cause you to realise that you've been doubting your abilities. The mind of no two people can function in the same way. You have the choice of deciding your own primary resource that can bring you to unbelievable success. Once you understand that you are the one who determines your destiny, you will determine your significance every step you make.

One of the easiest methods to deal with a problem is to discuss the issue with someone you can trust. Discuss your concerns with the person you trust and lay down all of the positive and negative aspects that are attached to the issue. If you engage in debate and argument on a subject, you'll discover the things you're made of. If someone else is saying something, you'll know exactly what you want - maybe it's the exact opposite of what they say.

It's a great method of separating your thoughts, and to determine the things that are deeply rooted inside your head.

It isn't easy to achieve. If they were, almost everybody would be successful on planet Earth. It's up to you to determine if you wish to be included among the people who have never attempted or, more precisely didn't give it your best effort, or be included among the people who are among the top-performing people.

Raise Your Worth

It is a dangerous game to be in because there is so much pressure to be successful and beat the competition everywhere we look. In this scenario it is true that there are more people fighting for the same spot as you, with some who are as skilled as you, while others have more experience than you. Therefore, the issue is, how do you distinguish yourself?

Raising the bar is founded on the belief that you must strive to be the best in your job. Look aroundand you will see massive advancements in nearly every area in the last few times. With the rise of opportunities in different sectors and the need for skilled and knowledgeable professionals has increased.

Although the competition is fierce but your talents and abilities will show through. Involving yourself in a variety of courses and classes will not only increase your confidence but assist you in your area of competence. A positive outlook on life is always advantageous. Take note of the factors that will assist you to become more qualified for a better position. Start working on it from the moment you begin your professional career. Learn about the many classes that can help you to establish your reputation as a professional. Then pick the one that matches your needs. Find jobs and careers that can help you develop your abilities and propel you into an unstoppable position in the near future. Learn from your parents and colleagues, look over and evaluate the skills which have brought them to the level they have, and decide whether you have these skills. If not, effort to take one of the highly-demanding professional courses that will assist you in advancing your career. For professionals working in the field there are an abundance of online courses that could be extremely beneficial. Learn about the market for your industry as well as its needs, and then focus towards acquiring the required skills.

So, you must make every effort to develop your abilities until you stand out in your class. Don't set small goals for yourself. Instead consider yourself a giant and work for a goal that is lofty in your life. You will only be an elite group of individuals on earth by setting a high bar. Don't limit yourself to what you can achieve. Instead, you should strive to be the best you can be by your abilities and knowledge!

Well-planned and healthy habits and a regular routine are essential to increase your level of taking care of your self as you are working to success. The first step to treating yourself as a resource is to identify your strengths and developing them by incorporating effective habits.

Health is important and you must ensure that you are mentally and physically well-maintained. Even if you're not, make time to make plans to aid in healing. Take part in exercises and find some new and exciting hobbies which can help you remain at peace. It's well-known that yoga can be a great help in the long run, and if you include some mindfulness meditation practices to your routine, you'll be able to boost your concentration in a variety of ways.

Your health can have a major influence on your capacity to perform at a higher level every day. When you realize that you're an important resource to yourself, you should begin taking care of your health. It's not surprising that your job and other commitments make you working, which leaves you with no time for an exercise routine that is effective. The fast food culture that's rapidly transforming our lives including fast food chains and takeaway systems makes life much easier for us, however it also has brought about a variety of health hazards. So, regardless of how busy it is imperative to provide your body with nutritious foods and drink enough water. Set aside at least 30 minutes to complete an exercise each day.

Make sure to eat as healthily that you are able to.

Another crucial aspect of maintaining your health and well-being is to get enough rest. The demands of your busy schedule could disrupt your sleep routine. Your shift changes at work, along with taking on a larger workload at home, could make you vulnerable to serious health issues that are all related to the inadequate amount of sleeping and relaxation.

Many people have tried and evaluated the benefits of using incantations too. The idea behind it is to find out what works for you and adhere to the practice. Therefore, putting your health first over all other concerns is how you can be able to take treatment of yourself.

Refuel Your Mind

The success of your business has more to do with you than external influences. There are many who can endure any level of pain when pursuing their goals. Others are unable to endure the rigors of the duration of a day. Your determination and perseverance are the result of the food you put in your mind daily. It's similar to the notion of manifestation, which says that you can make an event happen simply by thinking about it. The more negativity you allow to penetrate your body and mind the more negative energy you will attract.

Take a moment to think about the most recent time you felt low and less confident? If so, what was it that caused your feelings to cause you to feel this in that way? The group we choose to keep is a significant factor with how we think. Make sure you surround you with people who are ambitious yet confident about successes as well as the lessons they can learn from their mistakes. Learn from your peers Ask them on their stories, concerns, and the stories they have about their successes and failures. Learn how to get the most beneficial opinions that will assist you with your financial and management-related activities. When you think clear about your goals and by feeding your mind with stimulating and engaging material, you can maintain a an optimistic attitude throughout. A mind set that is focused on progress will never fail There will be some ups and downs but your attitude is what will allow you to stay motivated all the process.

Give Yourself a chance

Such situations can cause many feelings of discomfort because of the stress that they bring. Don't be so harsh on yourself and allow yourself to be given an opportunity. There are many occasions where you'll need to replenish your motivation and energy to keep up your efforts in achieving success. But don't set your ambitions above your personal satisfaction. It's all your decision, and the risk of compromising your mental health for the sake of achieving your goals is not sensible. When you're feeling the urge to take the time to consider it, and then rest for a few minutes. When you're ready to get back in the game and put in all effort to accomplish your objectives.

It may be interesting to see how crucial your health is when you're trying to achieve the highest level of achievement. The path to success requires perseverance and dedication If you wish to achieve your goals as others in your life have achieved, make sure that you don't sacrifice your health or happiness while doing it. Be persistent and focus on the things you love doing most. Do things that make the most out of you, and not those that take your energy.

Chapter 8: Experiment

Most people have known about Jack Ma, the Chinese business magnate. He is most well-known for his role in co-founding Alibaba Group, a multibillion-dollar business. He's an entrepreneur and philanthropist but also among the most successful individuals that you'll see in recent times. He once stated "if you've never attempted to do something, how can you determine if there's a possibility?"

People who are successful cannot be made quickly and cannot be defeated quickly. Being in a position that is highly desired can't be a simple job. It requires years of work and determination, but trying out with new methods can be among the most crucial aspects needed to improve your skills.

Consider a simple scenario like painting your home. Do you select a random hue and paint your walls simply because the majority of homes in the vicinity are painted with the same hue? I'm sure your answer would be a clear "no!' prefer to browse through a catalog of colors and select one or two colors that you like the most. But that's not all. You might also request the paint sellers to send you an example that you would love to test on your walls, and then see if it's great or not.

The idea behind the analogy is that If you've paid all your attention to choosing the color of your home, why don't you explore all the possibilities to brighten your day?

Why is Experimentation Important?

Many innovative ideas have been born through luck and experimentation. No matter what the circumstances the process of testing an innovative idea or viewpoint could lead to a wide range of possibilities.

It's likely that you've noticed that typically, those who are only beginning working in the field are eager to experiment and try different possibilities than those who've experienced a fair amount of experiments at the beginning the course of their professional careers. This is that when a person is just starting out with a future goal they want to reach and, in reality, could afford to make an adjustment right from the start. They are viewed as more likely to succeed over the long term. But, those who have reached a certain level in their life believe that they've got a lot to lose should they fail to succeed by trying an entirely new method.

The insecurity and fear of the unknown are real. It is not wise to put their life on the line up to this point, only to jump into a new idea which may or might not be successful. Here are a few of the reasons to be flexible and trying out new concepts is a good idea to achieve success:

Learn from Crisis

It is difficult to predict when a crisis will occur when it strikes with a hammer and a hefty force to boot! Life is constantly changing, people are changed and perspectives shift as time passes. The most difficult times are a great source of learning and have the power to influence a person's outlook and shape their minds by making them more robust and tough. Sometimes, unexpected turn have to be made, and in such tough times that your road to success will be decided. You find yourself in the position where you have the option of experimenting with new ideas or to see what is in front of you. A stubborn mind is the most destructive enemy to people. It's impossible to afford to progress if every obstacle is going to be a hindrance to you. A time of crisis can hinder your progress but it shouldn't stop you from reaching the level of success you are entitled to. In a time of crisis that you need to discover the weaknesses you have and begin to open your eyes to greater possibilities.

Uncover Potentialities

What can you do to determine whether there are more options that are beneficial to your future or even try to narrow it down? Think about working for one firm before being offered an opportunity with a higher salary at a different firm. Then you hand in your documents and the firm which you are employed by gives you the same position as well as a promotion in the organization. What happens when you confront an issue? It could have repercussions for a long time , if you fail to choose the best option. The main concern is whether a position within the present organization is more beneficial or if you decide to try an entirely new job in another company is better. However, the decision is completely yours to decide.

There are no doubt two options, but the main point is that if you don't step out of your familiar zone, you'll not be able to comprehend and gain a full experience as a complete. Although being a part of the team can provide the most secure protection, embracing an entirely new field of work could let you explore the possibilities of a different you in many ways. Discovering new opportunities is vital and is only possible by exploring new ideas and conditions.

Respect Changes

What you learn when you are in the business world or working an occupation for a long time is that change is the most frequent occurrences across all industries. The saying goes that changes are not permanent and is the only thing that can be said to be true about the existence of our planet. Being flexible in your approach to life will result in an outcome that is amazing. Different people come from diverse backgrounds. It is the individual you are that should be open to different opinions, as well as the way that people think. It's not good to be in a state of limbo and worrying when new concepts and ideas are implemented. How you take in other people's thoughts and think about fresh ideas is important.

Vanquish Those Fears

Even the tiniest bit of fear can become the biggest boulder that's waiting to create a huge impact. This is a feeling that is a lot of to do with your confidence and also what you think and the way you view yourself. If you want to be successful in any field is a must, and one of the most important qualities you should possess, and on that every successful person will say, is a high feeling of self-confidence. Humans have progressed throughout the years on numerous levels, but eventually, we've lost our connection to our senses. There are many who have a keen sense of instincts, and even achieve in their endeavors. However, no matter what the circumstance is any amount of faith will ever be able to stop someone from achieving the dream.

Everyone is a victim of their own fears. Certain people are afraid of dark places, others are afraid of trusting others while others are fearful of leading others. The list is endless. It doesn't matter the reason you are afraid but how you intend to overcome it that is more sensible. A lot of times people are afraid to speak about their dreams in front of others because they are afraid they'll be ridiculed. This is a common occurrence and has been observed by everyone from the youngest to the oldest. The key is that you'll need to create an attitude in yourself which will help you become much less self-conscious as well as more confident in overcoming every challenge that comes your way. Your views must be clear in the beginning. You need to know exactly what you're going to say. This is the reason you need to conduct an extensive research regarding the topic you wish to explore. The right knowledge is the most important factor to attaining that degree of confidence. Through engaging into activities that will help you develop, you'll be able to conquer your fears one step at a time.

Experimentation doesn't mean you'll share your ideas and discoveries with your friends and colleagues. Be prepared to be resistant to any new idea or conversation however, be cautious and strive to remain positive and continue improving your knowledge on your career or business. Experimenting with your knowledge can be very beneficial.

Chapter 9: Document

Thomas Edison, as we all are aware, was a genius inventor who was able to accomplish amazing achievements throughout his entire life. He has 2,332 patents and it was due to Edison that America was recognized for its inventions like the electric generator of power and the light bulb. the fuel cell, massive communications equipment, audio recorders motion pictures and more.

Edison was an unwavering believer in keeping journals, and he did it regularly throughout his entire life. According to reports, Edison kept more than 3500 journals, with notes that spanned more than 5 million pages. A lot of successful individuals in recent years have admitted to writing daily. Some of them include Oprah Winfrey, Lady Gaga Joseph Gordan-Levitt Emma Watson, Eminem, and many more. What is the reason keeping a diary is believed to be beneficial and one that successful people believe in?

Why do successful people keep A Journal?

Since the beginning of time individuals have documented their thoughts and the important happenings in their lives by writing the details in their diaries or notebooks. It's rare to find people who have done this to create an historical book however, they've used it as a personal record of their lives. Journaling is a method used by many famous individuals in the history of mankind, including Leonardo da Vinci, Mark Twain, Charles Darwin, Albert Einstein, and others. Let's review of why keeping a journal is a beneficial and vital practice that will assist you in reaching your goals.

Getting Things Doing

What we think about in our lives and how we implement it are two distinct aspects on the same coin. You've probably been through an instance where you are tempted to work for a long time on something, and you have all the plans put in place, yet you aren't feeling the urge to implement one of them immediately. The delay of work and the need to extend further are considered by some to be a good thing. It won't aid you in reaching your goals earlier! Journaling is an avenue to get out. In writing about your goals and setting reminders it will allow you to stay connected to your goals regularly.

Although you may have the most intense desire to reach the goal but there will be times that certain circumstances may hinder you from finishing certain tasks within a specific time. It is not always your fault for failing to achieve a goal within an exact time. Let yourself be flexible occasionally, and consider things step by step. But, one of the most beneficial things to aid you in setting goals to keep your focus in place is to remember the time, date and how you attained your objective.

Remember the most recent time you went out shopping only to come home to find you'd didn't have a certain item. When you think that you'll recall every little thingyou've ever seen, you'll likely miss a few things in the close. It's unlikely that you'd have missed one item when you had recorded it in a list. Thus, it can be observed that writing down even the smallest thing like an easy grocery list can aid in a significant way. So, you can see how journaling can assist you to accomplish your goals over the long term.

Notifying Important Events

In your entire life, you will encounter various events. Some are extremely important, while others aren't worth recollecting. In any case, writing down tiny details can help you recall important events from your life with ease. All you have to do is to go back to the date you need to go back and look up what transpired the day before. If you're determined to being successful, you will be interested in reading everything you wrote from the time you had no experiences in your life. Journaling can allow you to have an uncluttered mind, free of doubts. For example, if you are ever confused when working at your objectives, when you examine your journal, you'll remember the reason you began from the beginning. A strong sense of motivation is attained by writing your own personal journal. It's not only going to aid you in keeping an eye on all the happenings within your life that have value for you, but assist you in expressing your emotions once you've recorded those events.

Examine Your Progression

Writing down your progress is an effective habit you can implement into your routine daily to ensure you stay on the right track and ensure that you are meeting all of your goals efficiently. If you do this you'll have a permanent the record of what must be accomplished even if it is difficult to remember it all on your own sometimes. Noting it down allows you to stay clear of confusion and will be able to take the action needed in a timely manner and on time. Setting goals isn't difficult and, should in this procedure you have to revisit an event that occurred in the past You can be sure that you have all the necessary details in order and without any risk that it will be contaminated since you created it by yourself.

One of the most effective ways to gauge the level of his success by examining his character and achievements since the moment he began. A graph of progress showing lows and highs is thought to be normal since it's evident it will take an enormous number of battles and survival challenges on every journey. If you are a habit of keeping a journal and keep it up to date, you'll have documents that you can refer to. You'll be able examine your professional career and see the steps you've taken up to now. Through this habit that you will be able to see what you used to be as a person and the person you are today. Individuals who want to change their lives by studying their journal can know the relationship between their development.

Self-Awareness and Daily Thoughts

As we've mentioned in earlier chapters it is you who have the greatest influence on your own life. In that regard you should be aware of how important positive thoughts are as well as how keeping a log of your everyday thoughts can help you in many different ways. Recording the thoughts you have in your journal could aid in gaining awareness of yourself and help you establish positive thoughts in your mind when having a downer. So, writing your thoughts down will always be beneficial. It can help relieve stress for you when you have to talk about some issue or another, and you'll feel more relaxed after by putting your thoughts and feelings onto paper. The personal journal is similar to having a partner and you don't have the same urge to talk about your thoughts to others, or count on or expect help from anyone else. It will give you confidence in your own abilities and can serve to guide yourself whenever you revisit and read the pages that hold your stories about struggles and the way you've gotten through it. If you learn about how your thinking has changed through the time, that is an amazing reward for you. It will provide you with an awareness of your own self, as well as you will feel a sense of satisfaction with yourself.

Influences Your Mood

Your moods play a major role to keep your mind at a certain level. There are people who are not happy all the time in their lives. With the range of challenges that life can throw at us and their families, it's not uncommon to experience anxiety-related symptoms as well as an illness of depression. Mental health is extremely important and the health of mind can affect an individual's professional career. There are a variety of reasons why therapy and different counseling techniques have become popular in recent years. It is a good thing that the way society views mental health problems has drastically changed and to the good. In the event that you meet with psychologists about your issues One of the most common suggestions they'll give you is to write down your thoughts. They will ask you to write everything that you feel, and like doing in a journal.

Writing is therapeutic and may be a healing process for your mind. When you experience pain or a rage of emotion and there's no one else to discuss it with, you can communicate with yourself via writing and in a variety of ways to console yourself and feel better than you did before. If you're angry with somebody and you'd like to vent and often try to do it by confronting that person, you'll end with a major dispute and be more agitated in the end. So, a better option is to record your thoughts in your journal, let it out and feel lighter and happier!

The emotions can be complex as can your mood. There are times when mood swings occur that could be caused by reasons which you're not conscious of. If this is the situation, instead of trying to explain the situation to someone who won't be able to comprehend your message You could simply take your journal and begin talking to yourself. It doesn't mean that you need to keep your emotions in check and keep yourself from expressing your feelings however, it does mean that you write to yourself, and then when you revisit it you'll be able comprehend the topic you discussed and what you were trying to convey. If you read it again and don't feel content in any way, then, it is fine. You might try different ways to deal with your issues. Journaling honestly can help clear your mind, which can benefit anyone. Thus, all the aspects that were discussed in this article show how crucial journaling is. If you've not been journaling this year, it might be an ideal time to start writing for yourself immediately! The notes you write on paper today and even in digital diary can be kept forever without hassle. You are able to at your own pace record your tale of accomplishment that you'll be able to read later on. It could be worthwhile publishing it. Documents written down can serve as evidence when you have to use your memory for something. in the event that something happened in the past. You can flip through your diary and will find the truth. But, when you record your thoughts make sure you be aware of one thing. Do not add any type of fiction to it. Instead Write what you know to be real and precise. This practice will enhance your organization skills and help you become more committed and professional in your approach. Make sure you are honest with yourself and you'll see how easy it is to be able keep overview of your daily life and how efficiently you can put in the work for your best future. The benefits of writing can't be described in a few words because it is the method by which we have been communicating for many thousands of years. If you decide to make writing part of your routine, you'll be amazed at how effective it is in many different ways. There is no one who is a born writer. Your skills develop over the passage of time. Therefore, don't be concerned and start writing down your thoughts, and everything else important to you, so that you can keep it for the future.

Conclusion

The truth is that your actions have the power to define or derail you. Simply put, your behaviors will define your character. Establishing positive habits through learning the fundamental habits that most those who succeed around the globe are, will encourage you and inspire you to be more focused. The purpose of the book is to assist you in helping remain on the right track to success by adhering to a few simple steps and discipline yourself in the same manner that great athletes have achieved.

The importance of habitual behavior in one's daily life cannot be overemphasized. Things you conduct on a daily basis, from the simplest things like the food you eat or drink, or your thoughts can affect how you feel in a different manner. As your body requires intense workout routines to help keep your organs function in top health,, your mind requires the same healthy food and activity. Your thoughts will control your behavior, and you'd not want to create even one negative thoughts into your. But, in the world of competitiveness, the competition to become the best in all fields is so intense and quick that you could barely find time to your own needs. Being a part of a atmosphere of competition can be an overwhelming task. Every person has goals to achieve and goals to attain and it's up to you for you to reach these objectives. Every person's success is different. What could be a single goal for you may be a lifetime dream for somebody else. You might want to be the most famous person on the planet and someone else may desire to be one of the top-ranking or most well-known. Whatever the case the dreams you have are what make you unique and special.

Thus, gather all the information you require and be motivated by the experiences that have been told by some of the best individuals around the globe. Take inspiration from their dreams and aspirations, as well as the challenges they've endured to achieve the position they enjoy in their lives. Each story of theirs can be a teaching point, and you will gain the drive to follow in the footsteps of the others one day. The path to becoming the most successful isn't easy however, it is also true that it's not impossible. If you've have read about the most successful individuals, you'll be able to see how normal they are exactly like you. Remember, If they are able to achieve it, you can too! Be determined, brave focused, focused and most importantly, take pleasure in every second of your accomplishment regardless of the size or how small.

Dreams aren't quantifiable because they are distinct for every person. But, the intensity of the desire to achieve your goal gives the dream a lot of strength. The key point is that no goal can be small. Every dream is infused with an abundance of passion and desire and that's what is important. Habits are a vital element of our survival It is the actions which we participate with, even when there is no one to observe. Therefore, focus on improving your routine and soon you'll see the difference in yourself as well as the opportunities you are offered. By taking the correct steps with the proper mindset towards success , and your goals are not that far away. You can be sure that you will succeed and strive towards your goals with complete confidence!

Chapter 10: Replacing Bad Habits

"Make sure you don't make any mistakes. Bad habits are referred to as 'bad because of reasons. They impede our creativity and productivity. They hinder us. They prevent us from reaching our goals. And they're harmful on our wellbeing."

John Rampton

In this chapter, we're going to take a deeper review of different methods to remove yourself from the chains that hold you down. Some may call bad behaviors. At the end of this course, you'll be able to make a better sense of what steps you can adopt to make positive changes to eliminate behavior that does not help you.

When it comes to certain behavior, you might require assistance from other strategies instead of trying to tackle it by yourself. A good example is when you be addicted to gambling, drugs or even alcohol. If your addiction and routine behaviors are negatively impacting your health and lifestyle you may need help from professional associations and associations who are aware of exactly what they're doing.

Based on this, you might consider joining support groups in which you're in a secure space and feel like you are able to help others by providing an extra shoulder for them to reach out to or someone they can chat with.

Before you even think about the possibility of replacing your habitual behavior by something different it is essential to do a thorough analysis and think about the reasons behind why you feel how you feel about the behavior. What do you get from it? What are the benefits of continuing to follow the routine? What are the reasons you're compelled to change your habits today? Keep in mind that making this change with the wrong motives won't result in anything.

Substitute the Habit

Instead of going without a habit, you might want to substitute it with something totally different. This is called behavioral replacement, and it's exactly as it seems. Instead of sitting, you can sit.

to relax on the sofa from the moment you arrive back home, don your sneakers and take some exercise or a walk instead. Sometimes, it's very drastic to change your current activity by something that's likely to benefit you more.

The habit of sitting down should be replaced by some sort of exercise even if you're just beginning to get started. Set yourself micro-goals. These can be measured by the amount of time you spend or the amount of work you get completed. If, for instance, you're looking to get started walking, you could establish the goal of walking for 10 minutes every day, or to take the required number of steps. Make sure you start slow and build up the fundamentals once you start to become more at ease with your own.

Be aware that anything over the top isn't good for your health, regardless of whether it's healthy eating or intense exercise. If you've failed to be successful with the habit-replacement It could be because you're trying too hard, or you're using the wrong strategy in the first place. If you're in this type of situation, you should look to the plan you've identified and determine whether there's something stopping you from achieving your goals.

Find strategies to opt for healthier alternatives rather than reaching for cigarettes like, say. One example could include making a large quantity of raw, fresh vegetables which you can eat during the course of your day. A good moment to prepare this is when you are feeling the need to light cigarettes. If this occurs, you should replace the urge with one of these behaviors instead.

Try to replace harmful habits with healthier ones can be a good idea, as could cutting down on the temptation to eat out by taking off those running boots instead. It is better to choose a gym to get an enjoyable workout instead of settling for unhealthy eating habits like binge eating instead. When you are able to put all of these little routines in place gradually, you move toward the proper direction. Through the loop of habit we know that there must be some sort of reward for getting the behavior altered.

There's no doubt that there aren't all habits that is simple to drop. It is important to determine as quickly as you can with the reasons for wanting to make changes. When you begin to include anyone else in the picture, you need to return to the drawing board until you are able to say that you're looking to change your life that are specifically tailored to you.

You should wish to become stronger, fitter, healthier, more content, and friendly. Instead of focusing on what others have to say, you should keep your eyes on the reasons for making these drastic changes to your life. You may realize that it's time to reorient your life around certain truths and values you cherish most to you as an individual.

What's holding you back? Eliminate It

There are always negative aspects that will hinder you in the process of changing your habits that have been for a long time. There are usually negative influences that can encourage undesirable behavior due to the environment you're within. Examples of this are factors like the way retailers choose to stock their shelves. The things that can be attractive and could be harmful to they are always in shelves that are at eye level. This is one way that brands and marketers take place in retail stores and encourages poor behavior.

Another example is that candy can always be found at the checkout point. This happens since they are aware that once you're done with your shopping, the willpower is not as strong as you might have had when you walked to the store with a particular goal in your head. This is the exact same as the habits we have. If we're thinking about the elimination of a negative habit do we stop to look at what we intend to do to get rid of it? Do we take time to look at our actions from beginning to finish to determine what makes us behave as we do?

In many cases, when we are trying to rid ourselves of undesirable behavior, we just look at setting a goal or an end date that we'd like that the conduct change by, but we do not implement a strategy that is feasible in place. What exactly is an effective strategy? It's a plan developed after analyzing the circumstances to discover what the main reasons for our behavior are at the root.

It may be necessary to separate ourself from a particular environment to ensure that we're fully engaged and committed to making the right choice in our actions. If the motivation and motives are in place, the chances are that we'll do the same thing every time.

It's only when we decide to eliminate our self from the world that can be tempting to be enticed by that we'll be capable of making the needed changes to our behavior. Changes in your approach to achieving your goals of changing your lifestyle can assist you in removing everything that is hindering you in your life.

Reduce the Trigger Effect

When you consider all four of these pillars that make up an habit, if you cut down or eliminate one of them , it's easy for you to understand how your practice could fall apart. The trigger is one example of a suitable element to get rid of. How do we accomplish this? This should be a process that is practical. Understanding the psychological basis of a habit can provide us with an understanding of what changes that we must implement. The habit becomes repetitive due to Dopamine's release into the brain. It is an "feel nice" chemical that makes you feel happy. In many cases, dopamine isn't just released in the course of a habitual event however, it is actually released prior to too. An example of this is found in people who are addicted to gambling. They experience an increase in dopamine levels right before they make a bet and not immediately after a victory.

It raises an important question. Aren't all our habits similar to this? Is it the expectation of a reward that drives us act or is it just the rewards themselves? If something is appealing to us, and the result is appealing, the more chance that it will become habit-forming. It's the excitement of anticipation that causes us to decide to act on something we wouldn't normally act upon if the cue weren't present.

Eliminate Dopamine as a "fix" then the whole habit is ruined. Eliminating any habits' components makes the habit collapse, too.

There are a variety of alternatives you can make to get rid of the habits that are behind you. It is important to do some deep reflection prior to beginning. When you've reached that point and understand the reason for your behavior about, it's easier to tackle and reduce it to pieces.

If we are carrying out a routine It is the expectation of a reward but not always the achievement of the action in itself that prompts us to actually do something. The process of creating feedback loops has been covered in the previous chapter. To remind you that this is a process of breaking it down into pieces to comprehend the principle that drives it. While you're at it, however it's crucial to keep your beliefs, values and personal beliefs drive the process rather than the performance. Your primary focus should always be on becoming the type of individual, rather than on achieving an outcome you're looking for.

Other ways to make habits less attractive are by identifying what trigger the habit. This is what we've discovered as the cause of the loop of habit. Keep in mind that if any one from the 4 stages is removed, the behavior will not remain. Imagine for a moment the habit is a tabletop and that each of the reasons for the habit are one of the four legs. If you decide to remove from the legs the table will no longer be supported and is likely to be thrown over.

Take note of your habits by identifying habits that could be a part of your habit-making. There are a few of them like:

* Where did the behavior occur?

* When will it occur?

How do you feel?

• Who is the other person in the picture?

* Does it occur in conjunction with an earlier behavior?

The change in your behaviour must give you something valuable. There has to be some benefit to it, or else all you're doing is denying yourself.

Recognizing the Things That Make You Sick

If you are looking to break the bad habit and replacing it with better practices before you make any changes, you need to identify what triggers you. What triggers do you have as well as what do you need to take action to address them? Are there ways to get rid of each trigger? Be aware that if even one of them is eliminated, the whole routine will be a failure.

Repeat the process for every bad habit you wish to eradicate. When you have eliminated every trigger, make sure to replace it with a fresh one that can help you develop a positive routine in its place. Once you understand what triggers you You will be more aware of the triggers. Keeping each one in check will allow you to take control of the triggers.

After you've determined the motivation of wanting to let go of a habit that isn't working The most effective form of motivation is to write it down. If it's in a notebook or covered in sticky notes place it where will remind you of the main motive behind your desire to break the habit at all. Place it around the house in areas that you'll be able to view frequently. Think of places such as the mirror in the bathroom and the refrigerator or your laptop dressing table. Create a list of reasons that you'd like to change your habit by adopting a positive habit or removing the bad habit and substituting it with a healthier one.

How to Develop Habits

It can be reduced to four simple steps, as outlined in Charles Duhigg in his bestselling book, The Power of Habit (Duhigg 2012):

• Trigger, cue or trigger

* Lust or craving

* Action or response you choose to

* Reward for actions

An example of this is the fact that you're not truly motivated by the act cleaning your teeth. Instead, you are motivated by the satisfaction of having an uncluttered mouth and the desire to avoid problems with your teeth. Every craving is connected to an urge to change your external or internal situation. The way you think or think about the things you want is what will eventually transform simply wanting something into a need.

In response to these emotions, you can then decide to respond or choose not to act. It could be that you think about it frequently or even taking action to address it. The way you respond to the emotions you feel will depend on how driven you are and what's in the way of you from satisfying the desire you're experiencing at the moment.

What do you expect to take away from that experience in the long run? What's the reward likely be if you decide to take action on the urge? What happens if you decide to fulfill the desire that you have and take action? What's the biggest payoff in the end?

Rewards must satisfy the first desires that we feel. The actions we decide to do must be memorable enough that they will be remembered in the future. Every action we take will eventually be a trigger for a habit. If the action you choose to take doesn't line to any of the four steps mentioned in creating a habit, it won't develop into the basis of a habit. The removal of the first trigger will prevent the habit from ever beginning to develop. If you don't have a motivation for something, it's likely that there won't be enough motivation to continue. If the undertaking isn't easy, you'll be unable to accomplish it, and then the plan is a failure. If the reward doesn't satisfy your initial desires There's no reason to force you to try the same action the next time.

When you remove the first three steps, you will not do anything to encourage the behavior you're trying to eliminate. If you can eliminate all four of the behaviors It's very likely that the behavior will never occur again. The change in the cue and desire lets you alter the behavior and reward. The cue isn't always that is the motivation behind why the habit starts. Sometimes, the choices we make as well as the actions we perform are not conscious.

Chapter 11: Creating Good Habits

"Habit is the combination between knowledge (what you should do) as well as the ability (how to accomplish) as well as desire (want to accomplish)."

~ Stephen R. Covey

In this chapter, we're going to look at ways to develop healthy habits that is, the kind of habits you'd like to have in your daily life. We will discuss steps you can follow to create your ideal life built on healthy habits, rather than harmful ones.

Be Specific about Your Personal Habits

Habits such as "read more" or "eat better" are good motives, however, they do not offer any guidance regarding how and when to take action to make the habit a habit it. To achieve this, it is essential to be specific and precise. The more closely-connected your new behavior is to a specific signal more likely it are that

144

you'll be able to recognize when it's time to take action.

Instead of just saying that you'd like to "read more" you can tie it to your evening or morning routine. The new habit you have chosen could read like the following: "I will read five pages during my daily meditation in the morning." Take note of how you've specified the number of pages that you are planning to read and the time you'll read them. Instead of doing your morning meditation the way you were doing, you are now reading five pages of the book you've chosen to read is now your routine.

One illustration of "eating healthier" can be as follows "I am going to eat 5 smaller meals per day, and eliminate all food items that are junk." Being clear about what junk food you consume can reduce some of the temptations to simply go to a drive-through for your favourite burger or soda. It's going to require effort from you to cook every one of these five meals every day and will require making changes to your menu and the benefits of healthier living will be a nice benefit.

There are many examples which could be included in this list However, I'm certain you've gotten the essence of what you must be doing in order to be precise and specific regarding what you'd like to alter.

Steps Toward Habit Creation

Before we go into the more practical steps needed to create healthy habits, let's clear some things about the process of creating habits. A lot of people are believing that habits can be created or changed in a short period of time. Although this may be the case for small practices, it's not the typical. There are many habits that must be addressed daily in order to ensure that they are kept in check. Think about how an alcohol user goes through the day, constantly striving to keep this destructive habit from taking hold. Similar is the case of recovering addicts or anyone else who is working on their own recovery.

Even the most healthy habits of a healthy lifestyle can be easily broken simply by skipping two days in a row when you ought to do something.

As an example, you've signed up in a local gym and you've decided to get up an hour earlier in order to start your morning workout in before heading off to work. Everything goes exactly as you planned, until you realize that you are going to be up late. If your alarm goes off the next day you decide to push the snooze button to sleep for a bit longer. Your alarm is set to go off once and again, the snooze button is a into the hands of a bad decision.

Since you didn't make it to today, it's much easier for you to avoid tomorrow. But, this could be the death knell for your physical well-being. Think about the effort you put in at the beginning to get you pumped and determined to get moving; your present choices will send you back to that place all over again. This may not be the direction you're aiming to be If you're not loyal to yourself and sticking to your pledges you've sold yourself short.

Here are some steps that you can follow:

Determine What You Would Like to change and why

The first question you have to consider in relation to any habit you'd like to develop or create are:

* "Why do I choose for this?"

* "What do I want my payout for?"

* "How many sweat equity do I have to put up in order to reach the objective?"

* "What will I be willing to surrender completely in case I look for something better?"

One example could include someone who has decided that they intend to reduce their intake on smoking cigarettes, or are sufficiently motivated to quit smoking away immediately, and make an informed decision about whether the health of their family is more crucial.

This kind of inspiration could be the result of a bad experience with a health issue related to tobacco, like an intimate friend or family member confirmed to have lung cancer. The idea of the devastating consequences this illness could be having on the people closest to you or your loved ones might be enough to push you to take the right direction. It is at this point that I've witnessed smokers put their cigarettes down and give up right after that.

Find a person who is an accountability partner

Select someone who you are confident is highly reliable and can fight back and pull you up by your bootstraps when needed and who will not settle for small-minded excuses and will inspire you to be a better person at the same time. Whatever person you select to fulfill the role, be sure to establish the guidelines for the terms of your arrangement. If you plan to meet at least once a month to discuss your progress, make sure to note your appointment ahead of time and establish this as the top priority in your daily life.

An accountability partner does not have any obligation to you If they're a good fit, however, if they're able to and you can meet regularly, it's best to do so when you can. When you first begin the process with an accountability buddy, it could be beneficial to keep meeting regularly until you're able to be on your own and achieve your goals independently. In this stage, you may begin to loosen the reins a little however this isn't completely done.

Meetings may be less frequent but you are still constantly in contact with the accountability partners. There will never come the point at which you are capable of working by yourself. Many people believe they have the power and determination to complete everything by themselves however, they will likely see their motivation diminish when they no longer dependent on anyone.

When you have a clear idea of the things you'd like to change, write your motives and intentions as clear as is possible. Write them down. Let others know the things you're doing. Making it as clear as possible can bring people within your circle of friends including your family, acquaintances, colleagues and friends into the frame regarding your objectives. One way to achieve this is to promote your message on social media. Send it out to everyone whom you interact with and also explain the idea to those who are closest to your heart.

One example of this could be to embark to a detox for 10 days. However, the plan calls for specific food items and a of discipline. The best method to achieve this type of plan is to persuade the members of your family to be a part of it. This means you can encourage one another on, particularly when you're not feeling good, or even inspired to keep going.

Create a Habits Plan

Make sure you spend enough time doing this practice to reap the most benefit. You're likely to have a the list of your habits like in Chapter

1. Then, record the your habits you'd like to get started on.

When you start your planner, concentrate on the positive effects of affirmations, and positive intentions to encourage the implementation of the new habit. Examples:

"I will perform x behaviourat [dateand placein [place]." This type of sentence may be arranged in a "If...then ..." format.

"If I am able to get up earlier I'll make an healthy breakfast for work."

"If you have a choice between water and canned soda I'll choose the water option to drink."

The reason this kind of intention is so effective and effective is that the actions you want to take are linked with a particular outcome you'd like to attain. Similar to any goal setting method, the more precise you're involved when setting goals the more successful you'll be.

A decision made in advance is that when the moment is right to evaluate your options and make a decision based on a specific decision, your choice is already taken.

Do some practice "Habit of stacking"

This is like implementing goals. If you've set one goal Try adding another one to go along to the first. For instance "Once I've washed in the morning, I will clean as well as floss as soon as I get home." It is important to note that you have two routines that occur immediately next to one other. Another example could be: "When I wake up early in the morning, I'll go for a run of 30 minutes," or, "After I've had my breakfast and went to bed, I'll spend 20 minutes reading before retiring for the night."

One of the advantages to habit-stacking is that it can and capacity to increase productivity. It's due to the fact that the goals you set yourself are so interconnected that if you are able to control one, you'll be able to control the next. After several weeks of consistent dedication to these goals, you'll be able to take advantage of each for the price of just one.

Make It Simple

Make your goals so that they're so simple and simple for you to reach that you can put aside all the feelings of procrastination. We've talked about the importance of putting one small goal over another. The most important thing to develop lasting habits is to begin with small habits you don't even realize you're doing. Then, you can stay committed to keep going on the course you've chosen for yourself.

Be sure to keep track of your goals and the steps you need to take to reach your goals makes it simple to stay on track. Combining a variety of small goals can make a huge difference in an extended period. Imagine that you fill an empty glass with water by dropping a drop at a moment. It doesn't matter if it's just a single tiny drop that might seem to be insignificant, there will eventually come a point at which the glass is filled up to its limit.

Examine each of your little habits exactly the same way. Simpler and smaller routines are also easier to keep since they require virtually no effort to achieve. You're motivated to stick to on the right track and stick through because you're accomplishing your goals automatically.

Reduce Friction

The goal of reducing friction is cutting down on the obstacles that could be getting in the way of you from starting to work to improve your habits. It can help you maintain a habit you've started, but you find difficult.

Certain of these ideas have previously discussed However, hearing them over and over repeated will reinforce the general concept. Before you go to bed put your workout clothes in front of your bed so that when you awake in the morning, they are right in front of you. This helps you wake up by becoming habitual with exercising. This prevents you from having to get up to look at all your equipment. This can result in frustration and eventually procrastination.

Procrastination can be the cause of your habits regardless of how small and easy it is for you to complete.

Reduce friction by reducing what stands between you and your habits. If it's healthy eating it is possible to reduce some of the tension you're experiencing by ensuring that your fridge is full of healthy food items and snacks instead of unhealthful alternatives. Making healthy snacks to eat the next day is a good method to keep on your way. This means keeping snacks of dried fruit and nuts at hand, instead of getting enticed to add that chocolate bar when you're at the counter to pay. A well-stocked pantry of fresh, healthy vegetables and fruits will help to reduce or completely stop the desire can be felt towards the unhealthy sweets and cookies.

There are a lot of options to remove any obstacle blocking your desired goal. All you need to do is to desire it enough. It all comes down to the number of steps that are between you and the routine you must be doing. It's all about removing the steps. Make sure to cut as many steps as you can to ensure you are successful.

2. Two Minute Rule

Make an effort to change your routine into a state where every one of them is completed in less than two minutes. This approach is taught to people and used in order to become more efficient. In his bestseller, Getting Things Done, the author David Allen teaches you to break down the tasks you must complete into bite-sized chunks that you can manage (Allen 2001).

If you apply this same method in your routines, can you envision how this can be used to aid you in achieving precisely what you are supposed to be doing? Your routines should be so tiny and insignificant that they need no effort. The ability to accomplish this with your routines is a sure sign that you will need to cut them up completely. It could mean starting with a five-minute walk and then moving to the next step as you get stronger and more powerful.

You should be comfortable with the smaller chunks of your routine before you take the next step and add more pressure to the stress you're putting yourself under. You'll be able to tell within yourself when it's time to expand your current routine, and when you'll be required to hold back for a while.

Establish Your Decisions

Change your attitude and connect it to your routines. We are of the opinion that the smaller habits, the simpler it is to implement with success. This applies to our ability to take choices. If you look at micro-habits, your decisions aren't even a fraction of a factor. That's exactly the kind of thing you'd like to have. You don't want to make a life-altering choice regarding the formation of habits.

All of this can make you feel overwhelmed as well as feeling as if you're being pushed into the corner. In normal situations I don't know what I would do however, when I feel as if I'm in a bind or being forced into the corner, the first thing I'm likely to do is get out fighting.

If you would like your habit formation process to flow smoothly one of the least things you want is to be a fighter. Actually, you want an opposite result. You'd like to be at ease and confident in every decision you'll need to make in the direction of the formation of your habits.

Working on Autopilot

Autopilot occurs when you're comfortable and confident in each habit you've started working on that they can be performed automatically, and without even having to think about them. This is an excellent state to be, but keep in mind to be gentle with yourself. It is unlikely that you will reach this point on the process of habit formation immediately.

We've covered how some practices can be very simple to adopt without much effort, whereas others could require years before reaching the autopilot stage. Don't be harsh or harsh on yourself. This is a natural thing. You want to be able to go on autopilot for all of your routines as fast as you can because it means that your life will be a breeze. Let's be honest however, since most likely, this will not take place. It will take the slow route of inch-by-inch instead of being able to quickly take off your shoes for running and compete in an entire decathlon within two weeks of training. You must be honest and realistic about yourself. Be aware of what your limits and boundaries are.

It is possible to work on becoming a point where every exercise you do pays off and you're more powerful than before. This happens over time rather than occurring immediately.

Make Your Decisions Supportable

There are many ways will help you to reinforce your choice to make a habit of it. Some of them are listed below:

Combining tasks where the first one is linked to a habit. Part of this could be habit stacking or habit-forming by using"The "If... then..." ..." procedure.

If you are able to work to improve your habits for a set period of time at first and then, as you get stronger you can push yourself more by enhancing what you're doing. This will push your limits. Develop the habit of doing things longer and pushing yourself slightly harder. This is the way to improve your personal satisfaction with reaching your objectives.

Be sure to perform your routine as often as is possible or as often as you plan to complete it.

Reinforce your routines by being strict with yourself. Discipline is just one of the aspects you must be sure to have in place for each of your new routines. If you aren't disciplined, you'll likely struggle against any habit you want to strengthen.

Make it a point to up the ante in the way you reward yourself. If you're first rewarded in the first week and is a little when you hit the three month mark, the reward ought to be much more valuable.

Thank you for "Doing Nothing"

This is especially appropriate when you're trying to replace an unhealthy habit with one that you enjoy. One method of doing this is to reward your self with one day when you are completely unoccupied. It's different from this being a type of reward for breaking a habit that is harmful and procrastination.

Other options are to reward yourself with fun activities that allow you to take the time to unwind instead of doing what think you ought to be doing. Imagine how wonderful it feels to get yourself a massage on your back to thank yourself to stop drinking for three months. You'd definitely have the savings. The time you'd have would be spent enjoying yourself completely and rejoicing yourself for not deciding to do something or taking your time about it.

Chapter 12: Implementation

"First forget inspiration. Habit is more reliable. It will keep you going regardless of whether you're motivated or not."

~ Octavia Butler

After having discussed the process of creating good habits This chapter will concentrate on how to make them work employing a variety of strategies. Staying focused and consistent on the desired outcome throughout the process of implementing habits is essential to success.

Strategies for building Habits

In the last chapter, we examined the bad habit of someone who comes home from workand drinking a six-pack of booze each night, and

164

then sitting in the living room in front of the television. We discussed the possibility of replacing this habit by something that required fitness or exercise instead. If you needed to take a step back and examine the "why" of the original practice, given that it happened every time right after work, you can suppose that it was because of pressure at work. significant factor.

The alcohol was a method to ease tension and stress. In the same way, if we replaced the behavior with a type or exercise program, the result (stress diminution) was the same. Are you aware of how important it is to determine the cause for why you resorted to the habit first?

There are a few secrets for making positive changes to bad habits in the way that they'll remain in place.

Rewards for Successful Habit Implementation

If you are able to implement a habit which you've worked towards Make sure you give yourself a reward as quickly as you are able. Keep in mind that the donkey who does not get the reward in the final moments of the day is likely to quit chasing it. You must keep yourself focused on achieving the most important goals you have set The most effective method of doing this is to recognize and rewarding the achievement of a habit.

The rewards that you assign to your goals don't have to be extravagant or expensive. Instead, you should look for items that could be suitable and could contribute to your overall objective. One example is if you manage to stay at your gym regularly for three months. You might reward yourself with an exercise outfit that is new or a pair of sneakers for your gym.

The most important aspect is that there should some kind of reward associated with the routine that makes it a satisfying enjoyment for the user, instead of you working continuously towards getting something but receiving little in return. If you do not encourage yourself to keep going eventually, you'll be disinterested or bored when your motivation decreases.

When you achieve the goal you set make sure you give yourself a reward that is appropriate. This is essential because you'll be working towards an end with no reward to look forward to. The kind of reward you choose isn't necessarily extravagant or costly. You might have thought of buying an ebook, or you've even taken yourself to the cinema as an escape from your daily routine. Whatever the reason it will keep you focused and motivated to continue working towards your objectives. The psychological part within the brain, which is stimulated when you are rewarded. It will continue to motivate you to keep going.

Be Compassionate

Be kind to yourself. Instead of being judgmental and harsh try to learn self-love. We are typically more harsh on ourselves than others could be. Instead of being harsh with ourselves, we must accept responsibility for our actions. This must be done without feeling guilt or shame. You're trying to stay positive and focused as you work to implement positive practices into your daily routine and learn to master these habits. Self-judgment is a negative thing and can possibly cause us to fall behind because of the negative attitude. You have the chance to develop positive habits instead of dwelling on the negative continuously.

Be Patient

The process of developing new habits can take time before they are instilled and a part of our identity. Be aware of the length of time it's going take the new behavior to come to this stage. If you think your new habit is likely to be accomplished in the initial week, or two it is a lie. yourself. It is essential to have enough time set aside for every new habit, particularly in the case of several habits at the same time. Your patience is likely to be tested and you'll be required to stick to your routine as you work to make sure that you are given the greatest chance to establish your habits.

Start Small

Doing too much at once is among the most significant obstacles and shortcomings when it comes to establishing healthy habits. It's always thought of as follows: Your habit was not created over night. It has taken some time before it became an unproductive force in your life. It's only natural that replacing this habit with something that will bring you happiness will also take some time. Do not expect that changes to be made quickly. Instead, take the time you require to make each change happen so that you have the proper base to allow your small, gradual adjustments to take effect. It is possible that you will need to master the essential life skills like determination, self-control and the ability to put this into the practice.

Think about obstacles

Consider the what could be hindering your progress. What is preventing you from forming this habit? Most of the time, we're not prepared to put the full effort into making a successful habit work. A good example would being finding the motivation to get to the gym. You've recognized the advantages of maintaining your body and your mind in good shape. The gym might be too far away from home to keep you focused, so you put it off. A solution is to buy some gym equipment and work in the comfort of your own home. Once you've established a routine it will be much easier to think about going to the fitness center.

Be the Decisive

Decide to make a commitment to seeing changes in your lifestyle through the very end. It may sound simpler than it is. Making a choice to act and following it through to completion are usually two distinct things. The difference lies in the ability and perseverance to fight to overcome obstacles when they come up. Making new habits is always going to be a challenge that needs to be over. It requires the discipline required to see all of these steps through. Keep your eyes on those items that are the most important and just in front of your eyes.

Select Only One

When we take a moment to examine our lives, we find that there are a lot of our habits that we have to change or would like to change. Although being able to acknowledge that is an admirable thing, the person who really must revisit the same situation. It's better to concentrate on changing one particular habit at a given time rather than attempting to complete the complete "habit change" within a limited amount of time. Doing too much with several habits at the same time will cause you to be frustrated and could lead to a complete failure. Select one thing to tackle at each time, and when you're certain that you've succeeded in make changes that are successful by working on the first one, proceed to the next, and then the next.

Find Your Why

The practice of adopting healthy habits is well and right. However, you must be clear on what you're trying to accomplish. If you're looking to stop smoking, what's your principal reason for doing it? If you decide that you want to shed weight, what's your motive behind this choice? When we're certain of what we would like to achieve that it becomes much easier to allow us to establish the goals we have to achieve. It also gives us the motivation needed to accomplish whatever it is that we have to accomplish.

Develop an Support Structure

It is best to do this with your family and friends. Inform them of your plans to alter certain behaviors. When you do this, you'll find they can assist you and help you to make changes. Being able to count on them to help you will make the process simpler for. You can count on moral help from family members and your friends, however only if you've been transparent and honest with them about the behaviors you're trying to eliminate.

Practice Optimism

Keep your mind focused. It's only through using this technique to overcome everything negative that gives you the courage you require to keep easing anxiety. Positive thinking doesn't mean that you have to put your head in dust and pretending to be in order. It's about being able to manage your stress positively. Being focused on negative issues could make it harder to change. However when you're positive changes are more natural. Let go of the negative at the moment you become conscious of its presence.

Be prepared for failure

As you work to develop your new habits, you must be realistic and be prepared to fail at times. The best effort can keep you from a few failures from happening here and there. There's a saying that it isn't important how many times

174

you've been knocked down, as long is how often you climb back up. If you're aware that you're likely to fail a few times before you achieve success that takes the pain of failure. Implementing a strategy in which you accept every failure as part of the process will help you achieve success much faster. The most important thing is that you have a plan prior to beginning any new routine.

Change Your Routine

Do you have to make changes to your routine so that you are more motivated to make changes in your routine? Everyone has a regular routine, no matter if we acknowledge that or not. If you're looking to change your habits , you have to be able tackle them every day. One of the most effective methods to achieve this is to make these practices a an integral part of your routine. It is possible to incorporate some exercise into your daily routine (as as a means to ease tension) but only you'll know when the best timing to do this would be, perhaps in the morning, or during your evening routine. It's all about incorporating the exercise routine in a place where it will fit into your daily routine. After a certain period of time, you'll find that this is part of your identity and that you don't have to consider it.

Make Your Environment Ready

Have you taken the time to think about the effect your environment has on you in the process of the development of habits? The setting we place ourselves in has an enormous impact on how effective we are in forming or altering a habit. Consider these two scenarios as examples:

One scenario: We're trying to get physically healthy and fit, and we'd like to improve our lifestyle by eating healthier and engaging in more exercise, and removing any junk food items that can be an appeal to us. One of the most effective methods to achieve this is to get rid of junk food items like candy bars, cookies, chocolate sugary sweets, and other sweets out of your home. This is a method to reduce a portion of the temptation, by addressing the negative atmosphere.

In the next step, make sure you put your workout clothes on early at the beginning of your day, regardless of whether you've made an attempt to get to the gym or start slow with five minutes of walking during the day and in the evening. The time you do your exercise each day will grow over time, and once you get more fit, you'll soon realize that your time is getting longer. You'll be able to increase your intensity, and may find yourself running rather than battling your first walks. This is due to the fact that you've established a positive and healthy environment.

Scenario 2 Two scenarios: You're trying to reach the same thing like the one above, but you're constantly surrounded by neighbours and friends who aren't doing much with regards to fitness. Instead, they sit for hours on the couch, watching sports on television including all the food and drinks that are usually served with the excitement of a game.

Although you may be thinking to change your lifestyle and taking things in small increments isn't an easy task when you are in this scenario regularly. The time you spend watching sports on the TV may already be routine and could happen every weekend. However, regardless of any progress you make during the week when it comes to losing weight or altering your lifestyle, this is going to all be a disaster due to your choices of surroundings on the weekend.

This scenario would be like the alcoholic who hangs out with friends in a local bar. There is always temptation and the possibility of falling back into the old, familiarroutines is much less likely than, for instance, going to with the same set of people and attending a movie.

Think about the way your surroundings can be beneficial or detrimental to you when trying to establish or break certain habits.

The best part is there's a solution for you if you want to make these lifestyle changes. One option is to locate a place you can go to help you make the changes you're looking to make, regardless of whether this is a fitness boot camp, or healthy food retreat. Plan these out, but make certain that you're doing it with the right motives You should be motivated to make changes. Instead of making changes to please others around you You should be motivated to change things for yourself. If your motivation isn't top-notch, then do not even think about investing in this. If, however, you're serious about it, and can locate a suitable program to you, then these programs can provide the ideal environment to make changes.

Set Up Your Environment

Create a favorable environment for the favor of habit formation. Install everything you require prior to the time that you'll need it. Don't just wait until you're halfway through making an effort to create a positive habit to realize you'll need to make a change, or you're missing a component that you're looking for. Since you're focusing on the small things in the absence of making your home and environment ready, you could possibly sabotage your new habit completely. If that's the case, then you'll have to set your alarm for the same time in the morning to allow you to start your morning routines or go out for a run in the morning or workout at the gym, or whatever make sure you set multiple alarms that will wake you up until the habit is completely strengthened.

It is possible that you need to alter certain habits in order to create a more conducive environment. A good example of this is to make sure that you get enough sleeping time at night to ensure that when you get up in the morning, you are energized and ready for the day ahead.

In this case, you might need to to sacrifice some things. You might be used to watching a variety of films on Netflix before bed. Cut this down or incorporate it into a the reward system. For instance, if you wake up and manage to make it to the gym each morning for two weeks without a day off you can reward yourself by being allowed to watch two films on Netflix on the course of a weekend.

Make sure that the reward does not interrupt your routine routines. You want everything to to run at a smooth pace without the need to endure an unstoppable process with regard to your new routines. The only thing this will cause you to be frustrated and make you give up.

If you're serious about making changes in your life, be aware that it could mean altering your circle of friends. It's not something people want to be told, but you must be able to eliminate any temptations that surround you.

As an example Here are some suggestions that you could do to help you break your current behavior and change it to something positive

* Ask your family members, friends and other people you have a connection with to keep in touch with you on a regular basis to see what you're doing.

Stay inspired with blogs and magazines articles, and watching health shows on the television.

• Try to be a part of people who are taking the steps you're trying to accomplish. If you're looking to be healthier take a class at the gym or join a club that encourages healthy eating habits.

• Set reminders around you with sticky notes. Other motivational quotes can to keep you on track even when you're ready to give up. Set these reminders everywhere in your house: on your refrigerator, on the kitchen cabinets as well as on mirrors in bathrooms, and any other areas where you are likely to have to check often.

* Share the information with other people who you're trying to break or change your habits.

Try exercising in a group. This will help keep you motivated and will prevent you from skipping the day.

* We've discussed this before but it's an essential aspect to eliminate all temptations away from the home. If you're trying to stop smoking cigarettes, eliminate all cigarettes. If you're trying to stop drinking, eliminate all alcohol from your home.

If you want to be healthy when it comes to eating, you should prepare plenty of snacks ahead of time rather than waiting until you're starving and prepared to tackle whatever in the fridge.

Make it look worth doing

What exactly is creating a look that your routine is worth doing? Do you have the ability to make them appear attractive in some way? Perhaps the phrase "worth doing" ought to be replaced with making your new routines enjoyable. I don't know about your but I'd fight to get up from an icy and warm mattress early at 5.00 a.m. in order to go to the gym in the morning before everyone else gets up and goes.

How can you make fun of your workout routine? Think about mixing some of your favourite music into a group mix on Spotify or setting up your music player with tracks which you can blast while you're doing your workout. The rhythm and feel of your preferred tunes makes your workout experience totally different . There could be some pain points which you are able to work through just because you're motivated.

www.ingramcontent.com/pod-product-compliance
Lightning Source LLC
Chambersburg PA
CBHW060500030426
42337CB00015B/1672